BROTHER AGAINST BROTHER

Published in 1998 by
Mercier Press
5 French Church Street Cork
Tel: (021) 275040; Fax (021) 274969
E-mail: books@mercier.ie
16 Hume Street Dublin 2
Tel: (01) 661 5299; Fax: (01) 661 8583
E-mail: books@marino.ie

Trade enquiries to CMD Distribution
55A Spruce Avenue
Stillorgan Industrial Park
Blackrock County Dublin
Tel: (01) 294 2556; Fax: (01) 294 2564

© Mrs Liam Deasy 1982

ISBN 1 85635 266 8

10 9 8 7 6 5 4 3 2 1

A CIP record for this title is available
from the British Library

Cover design by Liam Furlong
Printed in Ireland by ColourBooks,
Baldoyle Industrial Estate, Dublin 13

BROTHER AGAINST BROTHER

LIAM DEASY

MERCIER PRESS

Contents

Contents

Biographical Note

Liam Deasy was born in Kilmacsimon Quay, near Bandon, Co. Cork in the year 1896. He left school at the age of thirteen to work in Bandon town. He was attracted to the various nationalistic movements, particularly the Gaelic Athletic Association, but it was not until 1917 that he joined the Irish Volunteers. This delay was due largely to various bouts of illness. He formed a company of Volunteers in nearby Innishannon and was elected its first Captain. His special ability as an organiser brought him to the attention of the Battalion Commanders and on the formation of the West Cork Brigade he was appointed Adjutant.

Almost from the time he joined the Volunteers he was 'on the run' and took part in several important engagements. When the Brigade Commander, Charlie Hurley was killed in action, Liam Deasy became the unanimous choice of the Brigade Staff and the seven Battalion Commandants to fill the vacancy. He held this command up to the Truce where this story begins.

In 1973 he published his account of the fight against the British in West Cork in a book called *Towards Ireland Free*. Tom Barry, who was only in the movement a short time before the Truce and who knew very little of what really happened in West Cork, took exception to a number of things Deasy said and wrote a rather hysterical pamphlet which was immediately rejected by a group of the surviving members of the West Cork Brigade. They issued the following statement to the press:

> We, the undersigned, former members of the Third
> West Cork Brigade 1920/21 wish to disassociate
> ourselves from the contents of a booklet entitled
> 'The Reality of the Anglo-Irish War 1920/21 in
> West Cork' (Refutations, Corrections and Com-
> ments on Liam Deasy's *Towards Ireland Free*) by
> Tom Barry and published by Anvil Books Ltd.,
> Tralee.
>
> Liam Deasy's book is, in our opinion, a very fair
> and complete account of the organisation and
> activities of the Third West Cork Brigade 1917/
> 1921.
>
> Signed: Ralph Keyes (Bantry), Denis D. Lordan
> (Cork), Christy O'Connell (Eyeries), Liam Dwyer
> (Ardgroom), Dr E. Callanan (Bandon), John Fitz-
> gerald (Kilbrittain), Dan O'Driscoll (Drimoleague),
> Sam Kingston (Drinagh), Flor Begley (Bandon),
> Seán O'Driscoll (Skibbereen), Paddy O'Brien
> (Dunmanway), James Crowley (Behagullane),
> Batt Murphy (Clonakilty), Frank Neville (Upton).

When the Civil War was over Deasy and many
others had to pick up the threads of their lives in a very
hostile environment. After a hard initial struggle, he
founded with a number of colleagues the well known
firm of 'Ideal Weatherproof Ltd' which became one of
the most successful industries in the young state. In
later years he became managing director of an
associated company 'Trimproof Ltd'.

More than once de Valera asked him to stand in
West Cork as a candidate for Dáil Éireann, but Deasy

felt he was too heavily committed to the building up of the industry with which he was associated.

On 26 June 1940 Liam Deasy, with many of his former comrades, enlisted in the Irish Army for the duration of the emergency. Within a year he had risen to the rank of Commandant and was appointed a Command Staff Officer Southern Command, with responsibility for organising the Local Defence Force. Within a short time he had brought its members up to 20,000 and had welded it into a powerful and effective auxilary army. In October 1942 he was promoted to the staff of GHQ in Dublin in the directorate of the Local Defence Force, where he remained until the war was over in 1945.

He devoted a lot of time in his later years to writing his book *Towards Ireland Free* which was published in 1973 and which enjoyed considerable success. He died shortly afterwards in August 1974. Before he died he completed the first draft of the present book but did not get the opportunity to revise and polish it as he would have wished. His family and friends, however, felt that it should be published, even though it might suffer from the fact that he died before he was able to put the final touches to it.

1. Last Days of War

In writing this account of my part in the Civil War, 1922-1923, I feel that a short preliminary chapter is necessary in order to put the subject into its full perspective. We are still very close to that sad period of our history and it seems to me advisable, as a help to future historians, that I should relate the events as I saw and experienced them.

The late spring and early summer of 1921 were for us in the IRA a time when we had every good reason to feel that the tide of war had turned in our favour. This could be said of the country generally, but particularly so of West Cork. In our area — the Third Cork Brigade District — twenty-two RIC barracks had been captured or evacuated. True, their garrisons had been transferred to larger centres but a vital source of enemy intelligence had been destroyed. The military were now confined to the towns and they depended on sporadic raids through the countryside, where their supply convoys and occasional patrols were frequently ambushed. Since our campaign had developed from defence to attack, our losses had naturally increased, but we confidently felt that the overall position had definitely turned in our favour, and we were anticipating a winter campaign which would bring us in sight of final victory.

There were three British regiments in our area. The Essex had their headquarters in Kinsale and garrisons in Bandon and Clonakilty. The King's Liverpool were in Bantry and Skibbereen while the Yorkshires were in Bere Island and Furious Pier. The infamous K Company of the Auxiliaries had a garrison of 120 men in Dunmanway. There was also a half company of 50 Auxiliaries in Glengarriff. In Bandon there were two RIC barracks, with others in Clonakilty, Kilbrittain, Dunmanway, Drimoleague, Skibbereen, Bantry and Castletownbere. At a very conservative estimate we were opposing an enemy force of 2,000 men with strong support available from convenient centres outside our brigade area.

At the truce we had 5,600 active volunteers enrolled in our seven battalions. Our armaments had increased from 18 rifles in 1918 and 30 in 1919, to a total of 130, together with one Lewis machine-gun, a large number of revolvers and shot-guns, two tons of gun cotton and 25,000 rounds of ammunition. A prime factor, and one of paramount importance to us, was the wholehearted co-operation and support of the people without which the War of Independence could never have been waged.

As the tempo of the war increased in 1920, the British Government was forced to realise that a military victory, if at all possible, would be a long drawn-out and costly one, and this was particularly unpalatable to the die-hard element so ably led by Lloyd George, the Prime Minister, and Hamar Greenwood. In keeping with their military tactics in the field, these two revelled i.. the vilest, bitterest and most outrageous attacks in public speeches and in Parliament. Lloyd George's references to 'the murder gang' and 'the small body of assassins — the real murder gang' together with his boast — 'We have murder by the throat', were ably backed-up by Hamar Greenwood, who as late as the 22 May 1921, boasted in the House of Commons that he 'would pluck the last revolver out of the last assassin's hand.' This was the general tenor of their rhetorical attacks, but it was becoming more difficult for them to disguise their true aim from the people of England, which was not to suppress crime in Ireland, but to suppress Ireland itself.

Consequently, feelers were being sent out to ascertain our attitude towards discussions on a possible truce. In May 1920 Lloyd George had told Lord Riddell (owner of the *News of the World*) that there had been a proposal for a truce, but he was against it. In November 1920 he continued his vitriolic attacks in Parliament and in public speeches, but now Cabinet pressure and public opinion led by two of the most influential newspapers, *The Times* and *Daily Mail,* were clamouring for peace and such was the growing demand on all sides that he gave way.

After his new appraisal of the situation in December 1920 he authorised Archbishop Clune from Perth, Western Australia (who was passing through London on his way to Ireland) to act as a go-between. The archbishop, whose nephew had been killed in Dublin Castle with Dick McKee and Peadar Clancy on the morning of Bloody Sunday, made contact with Michael Collins, and then with Arthur Griffith and Eoin MacNeill who were in Mountjoy jail. From these meetings there appeared to be prospects of further and favourable negotiations. Terms were tentatively drawn up but when the news leaked it was instantly sabotaged by the military junta. Sir Henry Wilson, Chief of the Imperial General Staff, and Sir Nevil Macready, Commander-in-Chief in Ireland, insisted that, given another six months, they would wipe out the IRA. Lloyd George agreed to this, but their boast was soon seen to be worthless and a trickle of emissaries began descending on Dublin.

It is also worthy of mention that on his return journey to Australia, Archbishop Clune called to the Vatican. There he found that British diplomacy was again at work. Pressure was being exerted on Pope Benedict to issue a rescript against Sinn Féin. With Dr Clune's assistance the Republican envoy in Rome defeated this age-old British ploy.

On 21 April 1921, Lord Derby, disguised in dark glasses, arrived in Dublin as an official mediator but his meeting with de Valera was treated as a mere scouting mission. In May, Martin Glynn, a journalist from New York, had no better success. Sir James Craig also arrived from Belfast and he too had an abortive meeting with de Valera.

In the same month a different tactic was tried when a Catholic Lord Lieutenant, in the person of Lord Fitzalan, replaced the militant Lord French. This gesture came too late but did serve to emphasise the growing anxiety in London. For the military junta the writing on the wall was so clear that in May Macready wrote to Churchill and said, 'Unless I am entirely mistaken the present state of affairs in Ireland must be brought to a conclusion by October — or steps must be taken to relieve practically the whole of the troops together with a great majority of the commanders.'

To this was added what Churchill had described as the 'despairing counsels' of both Wilson and Macready, who felt that if negotiations failed, military measures on an altogether new scale, requiring anything up to a hundred thousand men, would be needed.

This anxiety must have weighed heavily with the politicians for they knew that granting Ireland her independence would unloose a disturbing chain reaction throughout the Empire. In June General Jan Smuts had a meeting with de Valera but although nothing came of it Smuts, on his return to London, played a big part in the drafting of the King's speech for the opening of Stormont. This was the turning point recognised by all and was interpreted as a last opportunity for peace.

Following the King's speech in Belfast on 22 June 1921, his private secretary, Lord Stanfordham, called on Lloyd George on 23 June to say: 'Now is the time to bring about reconciliation. Unless something is done the effects of the King's speech will die away. There is not a moment to be lost.' On 22 June in a raid on a house in Blackrock, de Valera was arrested, although his identity was not known. Twenty-four hours later to his own amazement and to that of the whole country he was released without comment. This mystery was resolved three days later when he received an official written communication from Lloyd George proposing a conference with a view to peace.

Naturally this news was received with enthusiasm, particularly by the civil population who had suffered so much in the years of strain and terror. Yet, for us

15

who were fighting in the field it was viewed with some suspicion. In all our long history there were vivid reminders of England's duplicity. We had but to recall the Treaty of Limerick, the passing of the Act of Union, and the most recent perfidy when a Home Rule Bill which had passed through both Houses of Parliament and was placed on the Statute Book was denied to us. Small wonder we viewed the invitation with suspicion. The odds would be heavily against us with England playing, as we say, on her own ground, her diplomats with centuries of experience in such matters, so versed in subterfuge and chicanery, so very eloquent and practised in debate, while our representatives who came straight from the strain of years of terror had little but the justice of their cause to support them. It would be an unequal struggle. England would again, we feared, win the war having lost the battle. It must also be emphasised that at no time had the Dáil or the IRA asked for a conference or a truce. In contrast to the enemy anxieties as evidenced in their parliamentary and military activities, we continued on a quiet note of confidence.

I was indeed more fortunate than many in that I had been summoned to Dublin on a number of occasions and there I had the privilege of close contact with GHQ and I saw for myself the near perfect organisation which controlled the whole country. It was true, of course, that the arms situation was still critical, and that there were many areas which could offer little more than passive resistance, but never before had the country been so organised and determined to bring the struggle to final victory.

In October 1919 I had met for the first time, in Vaughans Hotel, Cathal Brugha, then Minister of Defence, Dick Mulcahy, Chief-of-Staff, together with Michael Collins with whom I had already been in contact in West Cork. It was a very informal meeting and we talked mostly about the war in our area. Many other members of the Headquarters Staff were constantly coming and going and it surprised me how nonchalantly they lived with the constant dangers all around them. The spirit of friendship and comradeship which they extended to me was an enduring link and a matter of great encouragement to me.

Next day there was another meeting at Lalors, Upper Ormond Quay, where Brugha, Mulcahy and Collins were again present. Gone was the informality of the previous night and in an atmosphere of military efficiency, Dick McKee's report on the Glandore camp was discussed in detail. Before the meeting closed it was announced that a Volunteer Convention would be held in Dublin for the main purpose of handing over control of the army to the Dáil, and it was arranged that Brigades in the country would send delegates to attend. In December, I duly returned with our delegates to this Convention together with delegates from some fifty other Brigades. The night before the Convention was to be held it was cancelled as the British had learned of it and were expected to take action. All delegates were ordered to return home. Later GHQ ascertained that these Brigades did agree to change the control of the army from the Volunteer Executive of 1917 to the Dáil and also to change the name from Irish Volunteers to Irish

17

Republican Army, which then became the official army of the Government.

In July 1920 orders were received from GHQ summoning the O/Cs of Cork, Kerry, West Waterford and West Limerick to a meeting in Dublin. We stayed at Devlins, Parnell Street, where Gearoid O'Sullivan and Sean Ó Muirthuile gave us details of the meeting which was to be held in a house in Marlboro Street on Sunday evening. We arrived at this venue independently.

Present at the meeting were: Terry MacSwiney, Dick Mulcahy, Michael Collins, Gearoid O'Sullivan, Sean McMahon, Rory O'Connor, Diarmuid Hegarty, Liam Lynch, Paddy Cahill, Dan O'Mahony, Jeremiah O'Riordan, Pax Whelan, Fr Dick McCarthy (representing Sinn Féin), and myself. Cathal Brugha presided. Here again we experienced the highly efficient organisation at GHQ. After a full discussion GHQ sanctioned our plan to continue the guerrilla warfare as outlined by the visiting Brigade Officers. We learned, too, that negotiations were afoot to purchase a shipload of arms on the continent and a landing site was to be selected on the coast of West Cork.

In December 1920, I returned to Dublin with Florrie O'Donoghue. Cathal Brugha again presided over a meeting at Barrys Hotel. The purpose of this meeting was to arrange for the importation of arms. We had recommended Squince Strand near Union Hall as a landing site and this was accepted. All plans for beaching, unloading and transferring the arms to Cork, Kerry and Limerick were made and finally Mick Leahy, from the First Cork Brigade was to travel to Genoa to pilot the ship.

Early in January officers of the three Cork Brigades met at Gouldings of Donoughmore where plans were finalised. Months later came the tragic news that the whole scheme had been sabotaged by British Intelligence in Italy. This was very disappointing, but had to be accepted as a fortune of war.

I returned to Dublin on 26 March 1921. It was a Saturday and I had Tadhg O'Sullivan with me. His brother Gearoid — Adjutant General, and Michael Collins met us at Devlins, Parnell Street. Collins told Gearoid to get a taxi and to our amazement and near dismay he took us to the reserve stand at the Phoenix Park Races where he mixed freely with the racing community.

At a GHQ meeting on Monday, we learned of a decision on the formation of the First Southern Division with Liam Lynch, O/C of the Second Cork Brigade and Divisional Centre of the IRB, as its first Commandant. This was truly a major development and there was no better indication of the happy liaison which then existed between GHQ and the Southern Brigades. To us, particularly, it was a significant breakthrough which would help us to develop the war from local level areas to a wider and more effective field. From Divisional Headquarters, columns and arms could be transferred to meet any emergency or to mount a full scale attack on the enemy. This was the unanimous opinion of the meeting and we dispersed feeling that the winter campaign would see us in sight of victory.

As further evidence of the close co-operation that

now existed with GHQ, a dispatch was received in mid-April calling a meeting at Lynchs, Kippagh, near Millstreet with instructions to bring Tom Barry, the Column Commandant, as Ernie O'Malley and Liam Lynch were anxious to meet him. It was their intention that he should train a Divisional Unit and lead it into action in outside areas, and in this way relieve enemy pressure on the extreme south.

There was a notable attendance at this meeting — Sean Hegarty, O/C Cork, Florrie O'Donoghue, Adjutant, Pax Whelan, O/C West Waterford, Garrett McAuliffe, O/C West Limerick, George Power, O/C Second Cork Brigade, Sean Moylan, O/C Fourth Cork Brigade, Andy Cooney, Humphrey O'Sullivan, John Joe Rice and Jerh Riordan representing Kerry, and myself O/C Third Cork Brigade. Liam Lynch was appointed as Commandant and Florrie O'Donoghue as Adjutant of this First Southern Division.

Subsequently, two sub-divisional meetings were held where ordinary routine matters were discussed. Then on 2 July 1921, I received a dispatch to attend a divisional meeting in the Clydagh Valley, south of Rathmore, where the first Divisional Training Camp was to be set up. Accompanied by Denis Lordan and Tom Barry we set out by night on horseback but when we reached Gougane Barra a message awaited us with orders to return to our own area. No reason was given and we were at a loss to understand what had caused the cancellation.

A week later, on Friday 8 July, I was presiding at a meeting of the Dunmanway Battalion Staff in the house of the local school teacher, John McCarthy of

Togher. This battalion area was one of the most important in the whole Brigade and the purpose of the meeting was the complete re-organisation of this Battalion and the appointment of Sean Lehane as Battalion Commandant. He was recognised as a well established leader of the Schull Battalion and his transfer to Dunmanway indicated anxiety that this vital area should be commanded by one of our most efficient officers

In the early afternoon John McCarthy hurriedly interrupted the meeting and showed us the current issue of *The Cork Examiner* which announced the cessation of hostilities and the declaration of a Truce effective as from 11 am on the following Monday, 11 July 1921.

The news was received in silence. There was no enthusiasm. The feeling seemed to be that this was the end of an epoch and that things would never be the same again. Even in retrospect, after more than fifty years, I well remember that my personal feeling was one of disappointment and I must admit I foresaw defeat and trouble ahead.

The correspondence which passed between de Valera and Lloyd George leading up to the Truce more than suggested that England was not even considering the establishment of an Irish Republic. We who, so to speak, had manned the front line and had fought imbued with the full Republican ideal and with greater hopes of success than at any other time in our history, felt we could settle for nothing but an Irish Republic.

In the light of what followed this may seem to have been a vain hope, but it was not without solid foundation. My own knowledge and experience of the military efficiency of our Brigade, as well as the achievements and successes of the other Cork Brigades, assured me that we were decisively winning the war. Nor was this belief confined to Co. Cork. It was also true of the Kerry, Limerick, Tipperary and Waterford Brigades. Since 1916 the three Clare Brigades had been in the forefront of the struggle, indeed relatively more families in Clare than in any other county were in the thick of the fight, with the Brennans and the Barretts being the leaders in that great county which never failed in a national challenge.

In the weekly issue of *An tOglach* and from other sources we welcomed the reports of victories and we sympathised with the losses and defeats — both inseparable in warfare. We read with pleasure of the successes at Ballytrain in Monaghan, Camlough in Armagh, Lisburn in Antrim, Trim in Meath, Clonfin and Ballinalee in Longford, Hugginstown in Kilkenny, Four Roads and Scramogue in Roscommon, Tourmakeedy and Kilmeen in Mayo and the daring rescue operation from Sligo Jail.

Since 1916 the Dublin Brigade had been active and in 1920-21 had carried out some of their most successful operations. They were fortunate that they were in such close touch with GHQ and not infrequently officers from it took an active part in attacks in and around the city.

Those of us who made official visits to the capital were privileged to meet many heroic men of the Dublin Brigade who were holding the streets against such heavy odds. On these visits too we met officers from other Brigades throughout the country and at such meetings there was always a feeling of optimism that our over-all position was favourable, that we could maintain our offensive and that Britain's position, in spite of the hundred thousand troops suggested by Macready, was becoming militarily untenable and in view of world opinion, quite impossible.

Although we were confident that the whole country was united as never before, we in West Cork had no illusions about the coming Truce. At best we considered it a breathing space which might last for three or four weeks and we intended to take full advantage of the opportunity to regroup and re-organise our forces. In this we were not pessimists but realists. We believed that England was once again at her old game of compromise, a role all too familiar to Irishmen and a role that bred suspicion rather than hope or trust in the heart of any Republican.

Our Dunmanway meeting of the 8 July 1921 ended at 1.30 pm and the Battalion Staff with the Captains from the thirteen companies, Derrynacaheragh, Togher, Aultagh, Behagh, Kenneigh, Coppeen, Ballineen, Bealanacarriga, Clubhouse, Kilbarry, Knockbue, Dunmanway, Shanavagh, dispersed without any great joy. They were however fully determined to face up to any emergency that might arise. Later in the evening Barry and I drove in a pony and trap through Coosane Gap to Crowleys of Trinamaddree near Ballylickey, the last Headquarters of the Brigade.

Here a dispatch instructed us to proceed to

Divisional Headquarters in Glantane, Lombardstown, and it also announced my appointment to the
Divisional Staff. Tom Barry was appointed Liaison
Officer in the area of Munster and Kilkenny for the
period of the Truce; an area under the command of
the British GOC General Strickland. Normally I
suppose being transferred from an area where I
had served in such moving times should stir up feelings of sadness but the startling news of the Truce
and what it might bring overcame all personal senti-
ment.

I contacted Ted Sullivan, Vice-Commandant of the
Brigade, and handed over control to him, and he, with
his usual thoroughness, arranged for a car from
Robert Kelly of Bantry to collect us at noon on
Monday. The car, driven by the owner's son, Mick
Kelly, left Crowleys at noon on Monday 11 July.
There was no ceremony to mark the occasion but the
Brigade Staff were there: Ted O'Sullivan, Flor Begley, Tadhg O'Sullivan, Sean Buckley and Gibbs Ross.
With warm handshakes they wished us Godspeed on
our journey. The drive was uneventful but there was
an air of unreality about it. I had been on the run for
almost two years and I was therefore constantly on the
move throughout our area, always on the alert in case
I ran into an enemy patrol. On this glorious morning I
found it hard to relax and to realise that my journey
was quite free of danger. When we reached Bandon
all feeling of insecurity vanished. No sooner had we
left the car when we were surrounded by people. We
saw then what relief the Truce had brought to those
who had suffered so much. To me this warm expres-

sion of their feelings was particularly welcome for I had lived in this area from 1909 until I went on the run. We paid a few hurried calls to good friends. It was the first opportunity I had to visit Con and Mrs O'Donoghue and sympathise with them on the death of their fine boy Jim who, with two other officers of the Bandon Company, was brutally killed by the Essex Regiment on 3 December 1920. Then I paid a hurried visit which was tinged with sadness to my father and mother at Kilmacsimon. Of my five brothers, two — Miah and Jack were prisoners in Ballykinlar and Bere Island. Ted was in Skibbereen, Pat lay in his soldier's grave in Castletown cemetary and only Jim, the youngest, was in touch with home. The visit brought joy and consolation to my father and mother. For them, as for the people of Bandon, the War seemed over and they could hope for brighter days and a re-united family.

Later that evening we continued on to Cork and stayed at Turners Hotel where Tom Barry had established his headquarters. As in Bandon, we were quickly contacted by friends in the city and it was a great pleasure to meet men of the First Cork Brigade who were now back in the city from the Donoughmore, Macroom and Ballyvourney areas. Next morning we called on the Wallace sisters in the stationery shop in St Augustine Street where the City Headquarters of the Brigade had been located throughout the whole period. Here we met the officers of the First Cork Brigade and had the usual bout of banter with the O/C, Sean O'Hegarty, who had lost none of his cut-and-thrust repartee. When he heard the news of our new appointments he immediately ordered the Brigade car with its official driver Jim Grey to drive us to Glantane.

We left Cork in the early afternoon in a beautiful Buick car. Jim who drove was accompanied by his brother Mick, while Barry and I sat in the rear seat. We travelled via Carrigrohane, Muskerry and Ahodillane in preference to the main road via Mallow, which was longer. Healys Bridge which was about six miles from the city had been demolished to impede enemy traffic and Jim Grey saw the danger too late so in an effort to clear the breach he increased acceleration. He almost succeeded. The front wheels reached the far side but the impact was such that Barry soared upward and over the side of the car which was a touring model with the hood down. He landed some sixteen feet below in the river bed which was almost dry because of the exceptional summer. The Grey brothers escaped by holding on to the steering wheel and I saved myself by gripping the front seat. We climbed down to the river bed and found Tom in great pain — one of his legs apparently broken. We were so relieved he was alive that Jim Grey jokingly remarked he was a much better soldier than sailor as he had failed to hold on to the rigging. We lifted him along the river bed to an opening and onto the road-side. In a little while a motorist arrived who was luckily stopped before he reached the demolished bridge. We loaded our casualty into the car and within half an hour he was back in the care of the Sisters of Mercy for the second time in eight months.

Sean McCarthy who was in Turners Hotel as

Adjutant or Secretary to the Liaison Officer, came to my rescue by providing alternative transport. That evening Billy Mackessy and Micky Roche drove me to Glantane via Mallow where I joined Liam Lynch, Florrie O'Donoghue and Joe O'Connor. There too I met for the first time Tom Daly of Firies and Ned Murphy, Mick O'Connell and Phil Singleton all from Lombardstown. In this goodly company I entered the second phase of my service in Oglaigh na hÉireann.

On 11 July, Liam Lynch had transferred the Headquarters of the First Southern Division from Coolea to Glantane as it was more central to his command. For the first few weeks we were the guests of many local farmers and some professional people starting at Mick O'Hanlons and ending at Lenahans, Castlemagner. The Truce brought no relaxation to Lynch, much less any kind of celebration. His one concern was how long it might last so that he could improve and enlarge the existing units and be ready for the continuation of the war which seemed to him quite inevitable. At best he considered this period as a brief respite of at most three or four weeks. From early morning his time-table of work seemed based on the assumption that six months organising had to be accomplished in as many weeks or even less. He drove himself relentlessly and expected a similar dedication from his staff. His expectations in this regard were more than fulfilled and he had their full and loyal co-operation.

Orders were issued for the formation of training camps, where a week's intensive training was supervised by staff officers.

After three weeks of great activity a house became vacant in Glantane village. This house was taken over by Joe O'Connor, Quartermaster, who very quickly had it fitted out as office, commissariat and sleeping quarters. From here a constant stream of communications was dispatched and received. Visiting officers were calling frequently with reports or for further orders.

This centralisation in Glantane could best be described as a Field Headquarters and gradually a daily time-table emerged. It began with breakfast at 8 am, dinner at 1 pm, and tea at 6 pm. Staff work continued all day often up to 1 am and then wearily we went to bed. The commissariat was simple as we catered and cooked for ourselves. Rations while ample, were seldom superfluous, as some of the visitors were wont to remark. Humphrey Murphy, that six foot three inch ex-Kerry footballer, now O/C of the First Kerry Brigade was plaintive rather than caustic on the quantity of meat supplied for dinner on his first visit. On the next occasion he took the precaution of calling to a butcher's shop near Lombardstown where he purchased a substantial sirloin of steak for his dinner. 'Free' as he was called, was a great soldier and a firm favourite with all. He was the best of company, always good for a song and able to relieve every serious situation by his light-hearted outlook on life.

All this clerical work was tiring to us who had been so accustomed to the active outdoor life, but it was so essential that there was no break from breakfast on Monday until Sunday evening when Liam would call a halt and suggest a walk in the countryside. Less frequently other duties would intervene and provide a welcome change in the routine. Sometimes it would be necessary to travel by train or car to Brigade Council meetings or to inspect battalions in Kerry, West Limerick, Waterford or one of the Cork Brigades.

In late August 1921 I had a four day break from office work. I prepared the itinerary for a tour of inspection by President de Valera and Dick Mulcahy who were to visit the scenes of some of the battles and ambushes as well as inspecting some 100 companies. This entailed a good deal of preliminary work for the time was short and the timetable tight. The tour began in Cork city and inspections were scheduled for twenty centres — Crossbarry, Bandon, Dunmanway, Kilmichael, Macroom, Coolavookig, Ballyvourney, Carriganima, Kilcorney, Millstreet, Rathmore, Barraduff, Headford, Drominarigle, Boherbue, Kiskeam, Ballydesmond, Clonbannin, Kanturk and ending at Mallow. The parades began in the early morning, sometimes at daybreak, in order to fit in the whole programme. It was a well deserved tribute from the President and Chief-of-Staff to the many units which had served right through the War with such success and distinction. Quite apart from the natural reactions of appreciation and enthusiasm which the tour instilled into all those taking part, it resulted in a rich harvest of new recruits.

This new life continued with the main purpose of building up our forces for some kind of confrontation that seemed inevitable. We had only a passing interest in what was happening in the Dáil and the correspondence which was still continuing between de Valera and Lloyd George was of greater importance to us and was tending to confirm our views that an acceptable settlement was becoming more and more remote. We were soldiers, not politicians, which is the only defence we can offer, if at this time our silence was taken as acceptance. When the initial talks ended and our delegation was chosen to begin negotiations in London we were still convinced that there would be no settlement if their stand for a Republic was not accepted. This to my mind was the kernel of all that followed, and in it the seed of the Civil War was ripening towards fruition.

Then came the tragedy. An 'immediate and terrible war within three days' was threatened and our delegation signed and accepted what Lloyd George called 'a just and righteous settlement of the Irish question'. In all her long history of aggression, persecution and intrigue in this country England had rarely achieved such a victory. By this iniquitous Treaty she tore apart a unity that, had it been maintained, was unconquerable.

In 1691 the position was not entirely dissimilar. England was anxious to make peace because of her commitments in Flanders where she was being hard pressed by the French. After a week of laboured bargaining the Treaty of Limerick was signed on 3 October. There is no more bitter chapter in our history than that which tells how that Treaty was violated. Yet, if Sarsfield had accepted the advice of his bishop and of the French, to hold out to the end, how different our history might have been. Instead,

with some 14,000 others he sailed out from Limerick–
the forerunners of the 'Wild Geese', an exodus that
has been repeated again and again and would be once
more in the aftermath of the Treaty of 1921. 'If
only. . .' How many tragic chapters of our history are
so introduced!

2. Last Days of Peace

When the terms of the Treaty were published in the press we realised immediately that, as we had always feared, England had won the war. Following on this publication came de Valera's denunciation and refusal to recommend the terms to the country for acceptance. This opened the flood gates of bitter recriminations and so followed the 'Great Split'. The scene of the conflict was transferred from Westminster to the Dáil in a debate which began on 14 December 1921 and continued in twelve public sittings and one secret session in the Hall at University College, Dublin. The Oath of Allegiance and Partition were there to remind every one that Tone's definition of a United Ireland remained unfulfilled, Emmet's epitaph could not yet be written and the Irish Republic was only a distant dream.

Liam Lynch, Florrie O'Donoghue and I had received invitations to the debate and there, day after sad day, we had our first political experience which was unforgettable and most distressing. We had to listen to men who a few short months before were fighting as comrades side by side, now indulging in bitter recrimination, rancour, invective charges and counter charges. Gone was the old chivalry and *esprit de corps*. Hearing all this meant the shattering of my many dreams, hopes and ideals pertaining to Ireland and her freedom.

As we were leaving the hall at the end of a debate, a

few days before Christmas, I met Dick Mulcahy who as well as being Chief-of-Staff was also a TD. I knew him very well and I also knew of the great friendship between himself and Collins. We chatted together for a few minutes and I then made a suggestion which I though might help to relieve the tension. I asked him to speak to Collins and recommend an adjournment of the debate until after the Christmas holidays. I did so hoping that in the season of peace and goodwill wiser counsels would prevail, tempers cool and a real effort be made to bring the country out of the unfortunate impasse that was leading to disaster. He agreed to do so although I never heard whether my suggestion in any way influenced the adjournment which was moved the following day.

However, the respite did nothing to relieve the strain which culminated on the 6 January 1922 with a vote of 64 to 57 in favour of the Treaty. There can be no doubt that many of the intemperate speeches made during these debates sowed the seeds of a terrible disunity, when only that unity which had brought us to the favourable position we held in July 1921 could have saved the day.

A Divisional Staff Meeting with all Brigade O/Cs in attendance was held at Glantane a few days after the terms of the Treaty were published, and it was the unanimous decision of this meeting to reject these terms. We sent a communication to this effect to the Chief-of-Staff. It was signed by the O/C, four Staff Officers and each Brigade O/C. This decision was not easily taken for it was critical of the action of Michael Collins in signing the Treaty and there were very warm feelings of friendship between him and all senior officers of the south. In addition he was president of the IRB and all the officers who signed the letter held positions of responsibility in their own areas in that organisation. During the critical days of the debate the Divisional Council had frequent meetings in Glantane and in Dublin. Early on we had forecast that a vote in favour of the Treaty would result. In fact some of us anticipated a larger vote than the ultimate majority of seven.

The tenor of the Dáil debates seemed to indicate that Civil War was inevitable. We in the Southern army were not so pessimistic, but events have shown that we were in fact unduly optimistic in thinking such a tragedy could be avoided. Even now, with full hindsight, I find it hard to explain our state of mind. After the vote in favour of the Treaty had been taken many and varied suggestions emerged. The main one, and the only one that would have been acceptable to us then, was that under the Republican Constitution the country could continue to develop and the IRA would retain its status and its full meaning.

Following on the resignation of de Valera as President and the election of Arthur Griffith as his successor many meetings of senior officers were held throughout the country with the hope of formulating a policy by which the anti-Treaty forces — which now included the vast majority of those who took part in the War of Independence — could co-operate with the new Government. In addition many conferences between officers of the pro-Treaty and anti-Treaty factions discussed various possibilities which would lead to such a working arrangment. The atmosphere was always friendly during these discussions since those with opposing views could appreciate the honesty and sincerity of their opposite numbers.

At one stage the pro-Treaty representatives — usually Mulcahy, Collins, O'Duffy and O'Sullivan — assured us that a Republican Constitution would so reduce the partitioned area of our land that it would be uneconomic for Britain or Northern Ireland to administer it. In this very promising atmosphere we agreed to the taking over of military and police barracks from the British and that the army forces doing so, irrespective of their political opinions, should retain control and possession.

By mid-February 1922 the divided military parties in this vital question of the armed forces were obviously approaching an agreement. There was no talk of a split or a threat of civil war. When the difficult question of future control of the IRA came on the agenda agreement seemed possible by leaving the issue to an All-Ireland Convention to be held in Dublin, on 26 March. The prospect was further enhanced when the Dáil, on 27 February, endorsed the proposed Convention and authorised Eoin O'Duffy to summon Brigade Conventions to elect delegates.

Meanwhile the first military barracks at Beggars Bush, Dublin was taken over and immediately an officers' training course was established there. Our Division with others throughout the country selected senior officers for this course which began in late February. Those who took part in the course subsequently set up similar training camps in their own areas of the country.

More by accident than design it happened that the second military barracks handed over by the British on 17 February 1922 was in Mallow. This, for us, was an event of real historical interest for it was the same military barracks, then manned by a company of the Seventeenth Lancers, which had been captured at midday on 28 September 1920 by the Second Cork Brigade led by Liam Lynch, the Brigade Commandant. The raid produced twenty-seven rifles and bayonets, two Hotchkiss light machine-guns, boxes of ammunition and a number of other weapons. These were loaded into three motor cars and taken safely to the Column Headquarters near Lombardstown.

What a contrast it was for Liam Lynch now to lead a company of armed volunteers through the streets of Mallow to cheering crowds with the British guard at the barracks' entrance presenting arms as he passed in. Many of the original raiding party were with him that day including two local volunteers, Dick Willis and Jack Bolster, who had been working inside the barracks as painters. Absent was Paddy McCarthy, that great soldier who, posing as the 'contractor's overseer', made up the trio on whom the whole success of the operation of 28 September 1920 depended. Earlier in that year Paddy had made a sensational escape from Strangeways Jail in Manchester and two months after the capture of Mallow was killed in action at Millstreet. He was the first fatal casualty in north Cork and one of our greatest soldiers. Lynch must have been a very proud man that day but he appeared as an army officer performing a mere routine act of military duty.

Meanwhile the divided parties, in what were now being accepted as the pro-Treaty and anti-Treaty armed forces, were on very friendly terms and most anxious to reach agreement. There still seemed to be no serious threat of a split.

However while these developments were proceeding with both sides working at top level for a satisfactory solution their efforts were being threatened by small dissident groups. Some merely protested while others went further causing minor clashes. Arms and munitions were being taken from one side by the other. Incidents, such as car seizures from civilians, further aggravated the situation. The most serious threat came from the Second Southern Division under Ernie O'Malley who had removed his Division with the exception of the East Limerick Brigade, from the control of the Dáil after the vote on the Treaty. Because Limerick city was a key position Eoin O'Duffy decided to take over the military barracks and on 23 February sent in his Treaty forces. Four days later O'Malley and Tom Barry led a force of sixty men into Limerick intending to rush the barracks but the plan miscarried, and they occupied other buildings in the city. A major crisis was developing when both sides received re-inforcements from outside and an armed clash seemed imminent. On 10 March, Liam Lynch and Oscar Traynor were called to a meeting at Beggars Bush barracks with Dick Mulcahy, Michael Collins and Eoin O'Duffy. As a result Lynch and Traynor travelled down to Limerick and, after much difficulty with both sides, succeeded in making peace. The following day the pro-Treaty troops were confined to barracks. All the Republican troops who had come into the city from outside marched out with their arms leaving the Mid Limerick Brigade in control.

As the election of delegates to the All-Ireland Convention continued, it was becoming clear that the great majority were against the Treaty, although the IRA, with the exception of the Second Southern Division, acted within the terms laid down by the Dáil. When Dick Mulcahy came to realise this trend he feared that the result would be, to say the least of it, an embarrassment to the Treaty party, and might even end up with a military dictatorship. The Divisional and Brigade Commandants assembled on the night of 25 March to prepare the agenda for the Convention but were stunned when they were informed that it had been banned by the Cabinet. In spite of this ultimatum, they decided to go ahead as arranged and they met in the Mansion House on 26 March. Two hundred and twenty delegates representing forty-nine Brigades of the IRA attended. All were anti-Treaty. This was an open challenge to the Government's ban and it was the first open break away of the army from its control.

Forty years later I discussed this crisis with Dick Mulcahy. First he made it quite clear that it was on his advice as Minister of Defence that the Cabinet banned the Convention. He added that at the time he was quite convinced that the Convention would form its own Executive and refuse its allegiance to the Dáil or the Provisional Government. This may be one of the imponderables to which no satisfactory answer may ever be given. I pointed out to Mulcahy that at that time the Government ban appeared to me, and to many other moderates among the delegates, as contributing one thing only to the situation, and that was to extend further the split that first appeared in the Treaty debate in December. I pointed out to him that there were at the time hidden elements which could at any time explode because of the ban.

Meanwhile the IRA was having its own problems with a group of extremists, some of whom would oppose any Treaty co-operation. Up to the time of the ban they were an insignificant minority which we knew could be contained but the ban gave them a platform for their extreme views and they made full use of it. If the ban had not been imposed so dramatically it might have been possible for the Convention to transfer its allegiance from the Government to its own Executive with whom negotiations could subsequently be opened. In effect what happened was that an Executive was elected which in turn then elected an Army Council and GHQ staff. Liam Lynch became Chief-of-Staff and I succeeded him as O/C First Southern Division. The elected Volunteer Executive was widely divided from the outset. This was quite evident in its attitude towards Lynch. He was an acknowledged leader of proven worth and integrity, with the Republic as his guiding star, yet, it now became only too painfully obvious that he was not considered sufficiently extreme by some of his colleagues. This unfortunately represented a clash between the moderates and the extremists. The result was many unpleasant incidents reflecting badly on the elected Executive. Worse still it appeared as if a number of independent armies were being formed on the anti-Treaty side. Such well-known Republicans as Rory O'Connor, Seamus Robinson and Liam Mellows could see no good in Michael Collins, Dick Mulcahy and Eoin O'Duffy. This distrust even extended to Liam Lynch, Florrie O'Donoghue, Frank Barrett and myself. We were regarded as being well intentioned but failing in our stand to maintain the Republic.

Although we were regarded as moderate, we felt that our policy was consistent and meaningful. Our one desire was to hold the anti-Treaty forces together in the hope that a Constitution would emerge which would leave all free to subscribe to it without the stigma of an oath to a foreign King. This kind of Constitution had been promised at the very outset and we had, at the time, no reason to doubt the credibility or integrity of those who had given that promise. In March 1922 the vast majority of army personnel was anti-Treaty and outside of Dublin City, East Clare, Donegal and Longford there was no Free State Army link on which they could build. Even in Dublin their position was insecure. The well-organised Dublin Brigade was commanded by Oscar Traynor who was anti-Treaty, and he was supported by four Battalion Commandants, Paddy Houlihan, Frank Henderson, Joe O'Connor and Sean Dowling. Andy McDonnell, who was Commandant of the Sixth Battalion in the newly formed Second Dublin Brigade, was also anti-Treaty. This Dublin opposition was, for the Treaty party, a formidable one. It was true of course that the majority of the active service units in the city, as well as intelligence units, took the Treaty side chiefly out of loyalty to their leader, Michael Collins.

After the convention, held on 26 March, a second meeting was held in order to confirm what had been done since the original meeting. On 9 April a third meeting was called specially to approve or reject certain proposals concerning the merging of the two armies. A motion was put to the Convention that an agreed Army Council and GHQ staff should be appointed for the purpose. On a show of hands the voting was approximately 140 to 115 against the acceptance of the motion. Immediately Tom Barry proposed an alternative motion that the Executive declare or resume war with England. In this he was supported by Liam Mellows, Rory O'Connor, Sean McBride and others. I moved a direct negative and I was supported by Liam Lynch, Florrie O'Donoghue, Sean Hegarty, Humphrey Murphy and Frank Barrett who had also supported the first motion on army unity. Cathal Brugha also supported us though voting against the original motion. Again on a show of hands Barry's motion was carried by 140 to 118. From the platform we could see men entering the hall under what we thought to be suspicious circumstances. The Convention had been in session for two hours and it seemed obvious to us that some packing of votes was taking place.(Many years later the late Andy Cooney confirmed that some 20-30 voters had been admitted without credentials.) After a short discussion the demand for a re-check was agreed and the poll then resulted in 118 against the war motion and 98 in favour. There was an immediate and tragic sequel to the vote. Sean McBride invited the delegates who had voted in support of the war motion to leave with him. Practically all those who had voted for war followed him, including Seamus Robinson, Liam Mellows and Rory O'Connor from the platform. On 14 April this breakaway body occupied the Four Courts, and next day they occupied Kilmainham Jail. The gathering clouds were dark and menacing.

On the morning of the 15 April Liam Lynch, Sean Lehane and I went along to the Four Courts to arrange an exchange of rifles from the Cork Brigades which were to be sent north to areas along the Border. In exchange for these we were to receive British rifles which had been supplied to the Free State Army and which would be forwarded to the Cork Brigades. When we arrived at the Four Courts we found the gates locked and a notice informed us that Volunteer Officers who had voted against the war resolution of the previous day would not be admitted. We read this notice with amazement and dismay. There was now a real split in the anti-Treaty forces. We returned sadly to Barrys Hotel and there we informed those colleagues of ours who were still in Dublin of this new situation. A formal meeting was held in the hotel and Liam Lynch was appointed Chief-of-Staff of the anti-Treaty forces outside the Four Courts. With bitter memories of the Treaty debate still in our minds this further division caused even deeper despondancy and seemed to destroy any hope of uniting an Irish army to meet the threatening crisis.

I left Lynch at his headquarters in Barrys and I returned to Mallow to deal with the accumulated work of the First Southern Division. The weeks that followed in the south passed without serious incident but the shadow of the Four Courts was ever present and seemed to forebode a coming disaster. The Pact General Election of 16 June passed off quietly, despite isolated attempts to break up pro-Treaty meetings and there was some obstruction at a few of the polling booths. I took no part in this election beyond registering my vote in Bandon.

The result showed a swing in West, Mid- and North Cork in favour of the Treaty, yet, this had little effect on the feelings and morale of the Republican Army. This should not be wondered at. From the first by-election in 1917 we were never unduly influenced by election results. Our mission was to continue the Fenian policy, to rouse the country and to strive for its freedom. In our generation 'the voice of the people' as expressed by the Irish parliamentary party at Westminster was a spent force and the people were gradually but slowly coming to realise that nation-hood would never be won by talk only. It had to be fought for, no matter what the cost. Once this was accepted the people enthusiastically took the cause to heart. We on our part felt that we could count on this loyal and generous support in winning the struggle for full freedom.

It may be that we were expecting too much from people who had suffered so greatly and who now felt that peace, even without full freedom, was what they really wanted. In the War of Independence the people had suffered the full rigours of a terror campaign and we could not blame them if they now wished for peace. They were also undoubtedly influenced by their economic position. In the absence of markets and fairs they had continued to provide us with food and shelter without any material compensation. They gave their sons to the IRA and their daughters to the Cumann na mBan. No people could have been so brave and so generous. It may be that we had come to take all this for granted and too many of us were inclined to bask in the sunshine of hero-worship.

After my return from Dublin I spent most of this time at our headquarters in Mallow Barracks. The days passed in routine work and I can honestly say, that however dark the horizon, we just could not envisage a Civil War. There were some few incidents when the Free State authorities began recruiting for their army. In the Second Cork and Kerry Brigades some efforts were made to prevent intending recruits going to Dublin. This did not seem very serious at the time because no prominent officer had gone over to the Free State side. Outside of our own area, however, there were many incidents. Sniping, shooting and arrests were becoming too common in Dublin. General 'Ginger' O'Connell was kidnapped and brought to the Four Courts as a prisoner. As a reprisal Leo Henderson of the Four Courts staff was arrested and this strained relations almost to breaking point. What seemed to have begun as a casual drift rapidly became a flowing tide which engulfed us all.

In Mallow, in spite of these daily reports, I could not accept that Civil War was inevitable. It seemed impossible that men who, only a few short months ago were so closely united in the common cause, should over-night, become deadly enemies. It became evident that many of my way of thinking were trying hard to avert the final catastrophe but the split in our own forces weakened our efforts.

The locking of the Four Courts' gates and the exclusion of Liam Lynch was a hard pill to swallow. He continued to operate from his headquarters in Dublin and enjoyed the loyalty of those who represented the majority of the Republican Army. He had transferred his headquarters from Barrys to the Clarence Hotel where he had among his permanent staff Maurice Twomey, Dick Barrett and Dan O'Leary, who had left the Four Courts. Early on the morning of 27 June Lynch phoned me in Mallow from the Clarence to come to Dublin on the next train. He emphasised that the matter was of the utmost importance, hinting that there was an approach from the Four Courts.

He met me on arrival at Kingsbridge (now Heuston) Station and told me that Liam Mellows and Joe McKelvey had asked him to arrange a meeting immediately on my arrival. We went directly to the Four Courts from the station where we were met by Mellows and McKelvey. They took us to a quiet room where we talked until shortly after midnight and then we crossed over to the Clarence Hotel where Twomey, Barrett and O'Leary were waiting. Liam told them that we had healed the split between ourselves, the Executive members, and the garrison of the Four Courts. He added that he had resumed his role as Chief-of-Staff of the whole anti-Treaty Army and that if the Free State Army were to force a Civil War the re-united anti-Treaty forces would resist by every means at its disposal. Dick Barrett's welcome for the news was expressed in brief words: 'In view of this reapproachment I am returning immediately to the Four Courts.' Moss appealed to Dick to stay with them, and reasoned with him that if war came, there was much more important work to do outside rather than inside the Four Courts. Dick remained adamant and went off alone to his comrades in the Four Courts. Later he was taken prisoner and finally executed with Rory O'Connor, Liam Mellows and Joe McKelvey on 8 December 1922.

Beyond the bald statement that our army was re-united and that Liam Lynch had resumed his office as the commanding officer I regret that memory now fails me in filling in the full details of that night.

Before leaving for the Four Courts, Mellows told us they were expecting an attack by Free State forces probably before morning. We were both sceptical and could not believe that Collins would attack, but both Mellows and McKelvey insisted that the preparations by the Free State indicated an early attack, adding that someone in the higher echelons of the Provisional Government had leaked the information.

Liam Lynch and I had a final chat before retiring to bed about two o'clock. I was quite confident that there was no immediate danger of war so I quickly dropped off to sleep.

The next thing I remember is that I was being roused by Lynch and I heard him saying: 'Do you not hear the shelling? The Free State Army has been bombarding the Four Courts for the past two hours.' I glanced at my watch. . . it was just after six o'clock on the morning of 28 June 1922.

We were silent for a little while, both of us too stunned to say anything. Liam sat on the edge of my bed. For both of us it was the end of a dream. Gone now was the unity that had brought us to the threshold of freedom, that freedom for which so many generations had fought, and in those terrible moments, we felt this same fight had to be continued until the goal was achieved — now or in generations to come.

3. To Arms Again

Due perhaps to our optimism and over-confidence that war was such a remote possiblitiy, no proper plans had been drawn up, but here and now we realised that a council of war was imperative. Maurice Twomey therefore arranged for a meeting on 28 June of all available officers. Present at this meeting in the Clarence Hotel were: Eamonn de Valera, Cathal Brugha, Liam Lynch, Sean Moylan, Frank Barrett, Michael Kilroy, P. J. Ruttledge, myself and some officers of Western Divisions. After a brief discussion it was unanimously agreed to resist by force the Provisional Governement's attack on the Four Courts.

After the meeting we made immediate preparations to return to our respective areas. After a hurried breakfast six of us, Liam Lynch, Sean Moylan, Moss Twomey, Con Moylan, Sean Culhane and myself set off in two jaunting cars for Kingsbridge. At a short distance from the Clarence we were halted by a Free State patrol under the command of Liam Tobin and escorted to the Wellington (now Griffith) Barracks on the South Circular Road.

I had often met Liam Tobin on my visits to Dublin during the War of Independence and knew him as one of Michael Collins' chief officers, a man of sterling character and undoubted courage. In later years I have often reflected on that meeting on the quays with a friend whom the fortunes of war had placed in a most invidious position. Being the soldier that he was he had no option but to do his duty as he saw it although I am sure his heart was not in it.

We were only a short time in the barracks when Liam Lynch was taken out. We had no idea what was happening but he returned in a few minutes and it was my turn to be taken out without any opportunity of speaking to him. I was taken to a room where Eoin O'Duffy, Assistant Chief-of-Staff of the Free State Army was sitting alone. Indicating a chair across the table from him he invited me to sit down. Then followed one of the shortest interviews I have ever experienced. 'This war is too bad, Liam,' said O'Duffy. 'Yes, indeed it is,' I replied. 'Where were you going when Liam Tobin met you?' he asked. 'To get a train at Kingsbridge for Mallow,' I replied. He stood up saying: 'Ah, you had better be on your way,' offering me his hand which I gladly accepted and with this act of mutual friendship we parted.

We arrived at Kingsbridge and boarded an after-noon train for Cork but this went no further than Newbridge. On the outskirts of the Curragh we commandeered a Buick car which Con Moylan drove. We decided to go by way of Kilcullen, Athy, Castlecomer and Urlingford to avoid the main road via Kildare and Portlaoise which would undoubtedly be held by Free State troops. As we entered Kilcullen so also did a convoy of lorries with troops coming apparently from Dublin. They halted. We did likewise, and for a moment we stared at each other; then Con Moylan let in the clutch and we drove on without question.

It was now dark and when we were passing through Castlecomer we were held up by a Free State patrol. It was a friendly hold up. The officer merely asked us where we were going. There was no mention of the war which had begun some twenty hours previously. As we were about to resume our journey the officer courteously invited us to the barracks for a meal. Lynch demurred, but I reminded him and was supported by the others, that we had no food since our breakfast in the Clarence that morning. Had we not accepted the invitation and I repeat, it was a friendly gesture, we would have been spared a very embarrassing incident.

We were entertained to a very substantial meal and whatever tension may have previously existed quickly melted away. We spoke freely of the war with regret. We all shared in the genuine hope that it would not develop any further. It was now midnight and we were anxious to be on our way so we expressed our gratitude for the courtesy that had been so generously extended to us. One of the officers produced a large sheet of ruled foolscap and placing it on a small table invited us to leave our autographs as a token of the friendship and camaraderie generated during our visit. Without hesitation we did so and with warm handshakes all round we continued on our journey.

A few days later an official pronouncement from the Provisional Government stated that Lynch and I had assured O'Duffy that we were neutral, or at least were taking no part in the war. This was confirmed by the signatures we had signed as autographs in Castlecomer barracks. This kind of vile misrepresentation is often practised in warfare but between fellow Irishmen at that early stage it was something which I can only describe as dispicable. It was a sad epilogue to a night when the military and ourselves fraternised so freely and parted in such a friendly manner.

We left Castlecomer and joined the main Dublin-Cork road at Urlingford. Again at Littleton we were halted by Free State troops but after a few words we were allowed to continue. During this brief halt we learned this unit was part of the Mid-Tipperary Brigade commanded by Jerry Ryan of Moycarkey which had elected to support the Treaty. The other half of the Brigade, under his cousin Jimmy Leahy of Boherlahan, took the anti-Treaty side. Both men were very good friends of mine.

At Cashel we were again held up, fortunately by yet another old friend, Tom Carew of the South Tipperary Brigade. When he saw who was in the car we got the all clear and arrived in Mallow Barracks at 8.30 am on 29 June, the Feast of SS. Peter and Paul. After breakfast we went to mass and for the remainder of the day we were busily engaged in discussing, and taking stock of, the situation.

The O/Cs of the Brigades were summoned to a meeting and when it began present were: Liam Lynch, Paddy O'Brien Vice O/C, Tom Crofts, Adjt, Joe O'Connor, QM, Tom Daly, Asst Adjt, Ned Murphy, Asst QM, Mick Leahy, O/C First Cork Brigade, George Power, O/C Second Cork Brigade, Tom Hales, O/C Third Cork Brigade, Sean Moylan, O/C Fourth Cork Brigade, Gibbs Ross, O/C Fifth Cork Brigade, Humphrey Murphy, O/C First Kerry Brigade, John Joe Rice, O/C Second Kerry Brigade, John O'Riordan, O/C Third Kerry Brigade, Garrett

McAuliffe, West Limerick, Pax Whelan, Waterford and myself.

Many other well-known officers and volunteers who had been active in the war, and who were now prepared to continue the fight, were in the barracks that evening. These included Sean Noonan, Mick O'Connell, Jim Brislane, the two Meaneys — Big Con and C.J., — Tadhg Byrne, Dick Willis, Jacky Bolster, Jerh Buckley, Batt Walsh all from the Fourth Cork Brigade; Dorney O'Regan, Dan Shinnick — one of the first to fall at Glanworth — Tom Hunter, Leo Skinner and Lar Condon of the Second Cork Brigade. Most of these men were living a good distance from Mallow but they rallied quickly to the threatening situation.

Only one motion was put to this brief meeting. Only one decision was taken. That was a unanimous intent to organise our forces on a war footing, and to first capture Limerick city and so gain control of the Shannon crossing.

Before this first Divisional order had gone out, individual units were already on the alert. By late evening of that 29 June we received reports that the First Kerry Brigade had moved north capturing Free State posts at Ardfert and Lixnaw and were even then face to face with a large Treaty force in Listowel. A force from the Fifth Cork Brigade had moved from Bantry and had surrounded the Free State post in Skibbereen. Likewise, units from the First Cork and the Fourth Cork Brigades with another from West Limerick had encircled two posts occupied by, what in war parlance we must now call, the enemy, at Ashford

Castle and Broadford inside the Limerick-North Cork border.

A late night report that the force in Ashford Castle was commanded by Donncha O'Hannigan disturbed Liam Lynch very much. Not alone were they neighbours but had been very close friends and had fought together during the War of Independence. Incidentally, it was remarkable that Lynch a Limerick man, born at Anglesboro, became O/C of the Second Cork Brigade in North Cork, then O/C First Southern Division while O'Hannigan, a Corkman from Mitchelstown, became the first column leader in that very active East Limerick area succeeding Sean Wall as O/C East Limerick Brigade.

When Liam heard the report that Donncha was surrounded in Ashford Castle in a position that made rescue or escape impossible, he discussed the matter with us as one of prime urgency. True, actual fighting had not yet begun. But our commander knew, and O'Hannigan knew that he could not now expect relief from Bruff or Limerick city, and their unit in Broadford, some miles to the west, had already capitulated. Liam was very worried that a man with O'Hannigan's record should be forced to surrender to us. It was also a delicate situation for Lynch insofar as any leniency might seem an abuse of his authority in favour of a personal friend. As a way out I suggested that I should go down to Ashford and make some arrangements with our local commander. Lynch welcomed this suggestion and gave me full authority to act as I saw fit. Actually the solution was easy as our commander was a veteran of the War and co-operated fully in allowing O'Hannigan to leave with his men bearing their arms.

Having seen Donncha safely on his way to Limerick I could not help thinking what a tragedy was developing, and how much men of the calibre of Lynch and O'Hannigan might have done to effect a permanent and satisfactory solution, if only it depended on them. Personally I have never regretted any effort on my part to prevent the tension of war from spreading, and even at the most critical moments, this feeling never wavered. I am sure there were many on both sides who felt as I did. I do not think it would be an exaggeration to say that ninety per cent of the pre-Truce Volunteers were entirely opposed to the split.

When I returned late that night to Mallow and reported to Liam as to how the O'Hannigan affair had been solved his happiness and satisfaction were very evident. Despite many differences of opinion that were to arise later, we were now of one mind in our efforts to find some way to end a campaign which we felt was going to destroy a solidarity which was the only hope of peace.

Next day, 30 June, Lynch left for Limerick and with him the first contingent to enter the city — men from the Cork Brigades led by Dan 'Sandow' Donovan. On their way to Limerick they took Free State posts at Croom, Adare and Patrickswell. They entered the city from the western end and occupied New Barracks as well as other strategic positions.

Opposing them at the other end of the city was the East Clare Brigade under the command of Michael Brennan, with men from Limerick city and county who had taken the pro-Treaty side. Brennan, a war time friend of Lynch, was the O/C of the Clare Brigade, and O'Hannigan was in charge of the Limerick men.

Back in Mallow I received a message from Paddy Cahill of Tralee. He was one of th founder members of the Volunteers in Kerry but had been relieved of his post as O/C First Kerry Brigade in March 1921. The cause of his demotion was his alleged neglect to organise all of North Kerry and to have concentrated too much on Tralee and the Dingle Peninsula. Whatever truth there may have been in this allegation, it was acknowledged that he successfully organised Tralee and West Kerry with Tadhg Brosnan of Castlegregory. As a good soldier, Paddy accepted the decision from GHQ but not so many of his supporters in Tralee. I now had to deal with this problem as one of urgency.

We had to re-organise the North Kerry end and appoint a permanent O/C and Brigade Staff. In response to Paddy Cahill's invitation I, together with Humphrey Murphy, O/C Second Kerry Brigade, met him in Castleisland early in July 1922. Paddy was accompanied by Dan Jeffers and Paddy Paul Fitzgerald of Tralee. We quickly came to the point at issue. Paddy was very anxious about his supporters. At least 200 men including many experienced Volunteers, who had seen action in the War were all firmly united behind him following his demotion. They had also refused to serve in the existing First Kerry Brigade for no other reason than their loyalty to Paddy. I should emphasise that Cahill was not responsible for this disaffection and neither was he a member of the dissenters, but this disunity, now nearly a year old, was crippling the organisation in Kerry. Conscious of all this, and most anxious to provide a solution he put forward a suggestion that the dissenting unit should be incorporated into the First Kerry Brigade and be so recognised there as the Ninth Battalion under the command of Dan Jeffers. Humphrey Murphy immediately agreed with this suggestion and I lost no time in accepting it. This was ratified, Humphrey Murphy then became O/C of the First Kerry Brigade. In the Civil War, this new Battalion was in action in North Kerry and Limerick city.

I have highlighted the circumstances of the Tralee crisis as a tribute to Paddy Cahill's memory. He was a man with a very strong will. Those who disagreed with him called it stubbornness. An early revolutionary he was a member of the IRB before 1916 and was closely associated with Austin Stack. He was the owner/editor of a weekly newspaper, and in my dealings with him I found him a man of the highest principles and he was never actuated by any personal feelings, either of resentment towards GHQ or towards the First Southern Division.

In the months following the Truce there were however many instances of disunity and acrimony. In many cases these jealousies, splits, genuine grievances, call them what you will, contributed in no small way to the major division which eventually culminated in the Civil War.

The tragedy of the military situation in Limerick lay in the commanders of the opposing forces, and the intimate relationships that had so recently existed, not only between the commanders themselves but to a like degree among the majority of their men. On our side were men — veterans would be the more appropriate term — drawn from the Cork and Kerry Brigades under Liam Lynch and Dan 'Sandow' Donovan. Opposed to them were some of the best men in East Clare and East and West Limerick under Michael Brennan and Donncha O'Hannigan. These four men now on opposing sides had served together with great distinction in the War of Independence. Lynch, the pioneer in North Cork, was the leader of that sensationally successful attack on British troops in Fermoy in September 1919, followed by the yet more telling victory in the capture of Mallow military barracks with its valuable haul of arms and ammunition on 28 September 1920. Dan 'Sandow' Donovan, an experienced city fighter in the First Cork Brigade, also commanded the Brigade Column that successfully engaged the Auxiliaries from Macroom at Coolavookig in February 1921. Michael Brennan was one of Clare's pre-1916 Volunteers who, with his brothers Paddy and Austin, were first to take their stand in refusing to recognise the old British courts. He led the East Clare Brigade in many engagements notably in the Glenwood ambush on 24 January 1921. He was the first O/C appointed in the newly established First Western Division and as such was now the officer commanding the Free State troops in Limerick city. Donncha O'Hannigan was a recognised fighting leader early in 1920, making history by his successes at Kilmallock, Ballylanders, Dromkeen and in other lesser engagements. Quite apart from their personal friendship there was a deeper liaison between these leaders — that of comrades in arms. On many occasions the three brigades had co-operated in actions under their joint leadership. One such spectacular operation was the capture of General Lucas with the two Colonels, Danford and Tyrell, as they were fishing on the Blackwater River near Fermoy on 26 June 1920. The safe transfer of the captured General through the enemy infested north Cork to west Limerick and on to east Clare must be recognised for what it was, a remarkable combined operation in which all three Brigades fully co-operated.

A Civil War unfortunately unleashes the bitterest elements, where brother fights against brother and where the highest and noblest instincts of man are submerged making them the victims of insensate passion. We were to experience all these evils, although I still believe that this was something the anti-Treaty forces had not wanted but finally accepted as a challenge which had to be met.

All this was very much on my mind when I visited Lynch and Donovan in New Barracks, Limerick. They gave me a complete picture of the situation which faced them but with Liam's optimism, and this was something which ruled his life to the end, he felt that we could drive the Free State troops from the city. In my heart of hearts I could not see this being accomplished, and many old friends to whom I spoke while I was there, felt the same and had no great enthusiasm to meet former comrades in actual battle.

I returned to Mallow with a heavy heart, yet hoping against hope that men like Lynch, Brennan and O'Hannigan might find a common ground for agreement and avoid hostilities at least as far as Munster was concerned. We transferred our headquarters from Mallow to the much larger barracks in Buttevant, which had been the British Headquarters for Counties Cork and Kerry during the War. We felt also that this transfer would bring us nearer to the scene of operations. It was carried out immediately with the co-operation of the Fourth Cork Brigade whose O/C Sean Moylan and Vice O/C Paddy O'Brien were both away on active service. The O/C of the Charleville Battalion, Jim Brislane was with us and being a senior officer I appointed him as O/C of the barracks. In view of what followed later it was indeed a fortunate appointment.

On my first day in Buttevant Barracks I received a deputation from Cork city, consisting of Professor Alfred O'Rahilly, University College, Cork, Frank Daly, Managing Director of Suttons and Chairman of the Cork Harbour Board and the enigmatic T.P. Dowdall. I knew them personally and respected them for their support during the War of Independence. Professor O'Rahilly had at one time been a prisoner on Bere Island. They had come to explore any and every possibility for peace. They were particularly anxious to meet Liam Lynch and had hoped to find him in Buttevant. I told them he was in Limerick and that they would get every facility to go there and see him. At the same time I could not give them any encouragement or hope of achieving anything by their visit. I explained how the whole position was continuing to deteriorate. I pointed out that Lynch was in the same position as myself and unless they could influence the Provisional Government to realise a fuller sense of their responsibility and agree to some accepted formula without any dictation from the British Government, they were merely wasting their time. As a result of this interview they returned to Cork very disappointed indeed.

Many years later Frank Daly told me that he felt responsible for the speech which Collins delivered in Cork city on the eve of the Pact Election on 16 June 1922 which blighted all hope of unity. In defence of his action Daly said he feared that the many incidents caused at the time by the anti-Treaty forces would seriously interfere with a free election and consequently it would be better for the Treaty side to have no Pact Election. I had to agree there had been some such incidents but I also added that his informant had greatly exaggerated their seriousness. I pointed out to him that in the southern counties our forces were strong enough on 16 June to prevent the whole polling machinery if they so desired. He freely admitted this and acknowledged the fair and impartial way the forces of the First Southern Division had protected the booths and the removal of the boxes to their centres and had supervised the subsequent counting of the votes.

Nevertheless I did not accept then, nor since, that Frank Daly's advice to Collins was the only reason why he broke the pact with de Valera. There must have been other and more serious reasons and I strongly suspect that he was pressurised by the British

Cabinet. It had to be something of this magnitude which led to his decision which was in my view more disasterous than the signing of the Treaty six months earlier.

Meantime, many things were happening elsewhere. First in importance was the surrender of the Four Courts Garrison at 3.30 pm on the 30 June 1922 with such well-known leaders as Liam Mellows, Rory O'Connor, Dick Barrett, Joe McKelvey, Andy Cooney, Paddy O'Brien (Fourth Dublin Battalion), Tom Barry and other heroes of 1916. Before the surrender many units of the Dublin Brigade tried to create a diversion by occupying and holding strategic points in the city and attacking Free State transport around the city centre. All this was organised and directed by Oscar Traynor and Brigade Staff from Barrys Hotel in Great Denmark Street. The most formidable of these attempts was the occupation of the Hamman Hotel and adjoining buildings in Upper O'Connell Street by a strong force under the command of Garry O'Houlihan of the Second Battalion. His staff included Cathal Brugha formerly Minister of Defence and Maurice Walsh now better known as Fr Tom Walsh OP of Dominic Street. Heavy fighting continued there for several days and when larger attacking forces with heavy gun-fire were concentrated on the hotel the defenders held out by going from house to house. Eventually Garry O'Houlihan ordered the evacuation of the whole block and directed his forces to fall back to Parnell Street and to disperse from there.

The order was carried out by all but Cathal Brugha

and a small party with him who refused to surrender although the building was on fire and could no longer be defended. They held out until that evening when Brugha called them together and ordered them to surrender before the building collapsed. He himself remained with Dr Brennan and Nurse Kearns. Those who had surrendered stood in a laneway at the rear of the building which was crowded with soldiers. Then Brugha appeared at the doorway. There were cries to surrender from friends and foes but with a revolver in each hand he darted forward and fell before a volley of shots. These final wounds added to the fourteen scars received in the defence of the South Dublin Union in 1916 brought about his death two days later.

So it was that after eight eventful days the first chapter of the Civil War had ended with the death of one whose whole life had been devoted to the cause: a death which might be epitomised in two words — unrepentant — unyielding.

In these tragic days sixty people were killed and over three hundred wounded. For the second time in one generation the city centre lay in ruins and the opportunity of averting the final tragedy was now lost. Prior to the fall of the Four Courts many held that the country outside Dublin should have rallied to their aid. Only the South Tipperary Brigade made such an attempt when a column of between thirty and forty men under the command of Mick Sheehan marched to join the Republican forces at Blessington, but as the position deteriorated they returned home. To my knowledge this was the only attempt to join in the Dublin action. If other Brigades had rallied and taken part in the Dublin fighting I very much doubt that they would have made any significant impact. If an overall plan had been prepared in anticipation of the attack by the Provisional Government's forces it might have had a relieving effect but would scarcely have affected the final issue in the city. There was no such plan on the anti-Treaty side which would at least go to show that we had no intention and certainly no desire to be involved in a war of brother against brother.

Those were bad days for the more moderate leaders of the anti-Treaty forces. Other deaths followed on that of Cathal Brugha and perhaps the one that struck home most forcibly was that of Harry Boland TD who was wounded in Skerries and died some days later in St Vincent's Hospital. He had been a prominent figure in the Volunteer movement in 1913, an active member of the IRB with a seat on the Supreme Council and would most likely have been a cabinet minister but for his duties as the country's special envoy to the United States over the years. He was an intimate and personal friend of Michael Collins and, although he differed with him on the Treaty issue, he still remained his friend. He was one of those who had helped to bring about the de Valera—Collins pact in the previous May. Harry's death and the mysterious circumstances surrounding it was another serious blow to the moderate wing which even at this stage was anxious to and hopeful of ending the clash with some honour.

As well as being in the midst of the rapidly mounting crisis in Limerick city I also found myself faced with many pressing problems in Buttevant Barracks.

63

We still had control of all of the First Southern Division area plus south Tipperary. This being the greater part of Munster it entailed catering for an army in the field covering four counties. In addition to feeding them it meant in many cases supplying them with full military equipment. Funds were urgently needed to meet these mounting expenses and the obvious sources were to be found in the banks, post offices and in the custom and excise office centred in Cork city. With the help of experienced administrators this was carried out on army authority. The only daily paper, being published in the south, *The Cork Examiner,* was subjected to strict military censorship. Under army supervision all these operations ran smoothly and we were experiencing little difficulty in the area under our control, except in Limerick city where the position was rapidly deteriorating.

On 1 July 1922 Free State troops were in control of two towns, Skibbereen and Listowel, but both surrendered to our forces on 1 and 4 July respectively.

Following a meeting in Mallow on 30 June at which all Brigade O/Cs and many other senior officers were present, Lynch made preparations and next day, 1 July, he set out for Limerick with 'Sandow' Donovan in charge of a column from the First and Second Brigades. At that time it was considered that the occupation of the city would be a mere formality and with control of the Shannon the further progress of the War could then be planned. The Kerry contingent under the command of Fred Murphy, Tom McEllistrim and Johnny O'Connor were also on the march. They cleared Listowel after a stubborn resistance and arrived to join the Cork and Limerick sections in the city.

As early as 23 February O'Duffy had sent troops to occupy the city and they remained in posession of the jail, the courthouse, William Street Barracks and Cruises Hotel, despite an effort by Ernie O'Malley and Tom Barry to dislodge them on 27 February.

So it was that Lynch arrived to find the take-over anything but a formality. However, he did take over New Barracks where he established his headquarters and he then occupied the Strand Barracks, Castle Barracks and Ordnance Barracks. Shortly after Liam's arrival in Limerick, Dan Breen and Stephen O'Mara intervened to avoid a conflict, and they arranged a meeting with Donncha O'Hannigan. As a result of this meeting the two old friends signed a truce by which they hoped a permanent settlement would follow. This was signed at 6.30 pm on 4 July but when published in the papers the next day there was an immediate reaction by the Dublin Government. Commandant General McManus arrived with orders to cancel the truce. This definitely ended any hope of a settlement and at 5.30 pm on 7 July Provisional Government forces in William Street Barracks opened fire on the Ordnance Barracks and the pattern of the Dublin conflict repeated itself.

Firing and sniping on both sides continued for some days. When heavy artillery was brought in by the Government forces Lynch was forced to move his headquarters to Clonmel. By then he must have realised the futility of opposing artillery in street fighting, and he ordered a general withdrawal on 18 July.

A defence line extending from Kilmallock to Bruree was established in the hope of holding the south but by mid-August this was broken and a disorderly retreat followed. Men were constantly arriving at Buttevant Barracks en route to their home areas in the First, Third and Fifth Cork Brigades and to the First and Second Kerry Brigades. In these days of crisis Jim Brislane proved himself an officer of outstanding ability, fully justifying his appointment as O/C of the barracks. The constant stream of Volunteers retreating from Limerick and Kilmallock were sadly dejected and in a bad mood. To meet this dangerous situation Brislane closed all the public houses in the town. All troops were confined to barracks until clearance was given for them to travel to their respective areas. For hours on end Jim stood fully armed at the main gates of the barracks and established a sense of discipline which saved much looting and other dangerous situations. In a few days hardly any men were left.

Brislane and his staff, Paddy O'Brien, Tom Crofts, Tom Daly and myself decided to evacuate Buttevant: before doing so, however, we decided to destroy the barracks rather than leave it for the Free State troops. Jim was given this task but unfortunately it was nipped in the bud when he walked into a Free State patrol which had moved quickly from Charleville and was probing its way into north Cork. This Free State column was commanded by two officers who were both good friends of Brislane. Denny Galvin from Knockgoshel who had fought in the same Brigade and Liam Fraher who had served in the East Limerick Brigade. Knowing Jim's rank and importance they considered him an important capture and took him with them to a billet they secured in Liscarroll.

Liam Fraher's account of an incident that followed is so humorous that it seems worth recalling and I give it in his own words. 'We took Jim Brislane into Liscarroll where we shared a temporary billet for the night. Next day, 15 August, being a church holiday, Denny Galvin and myself took our prisoner to mass at 10.30 am. We had a good central position and well up in the front of the church and Jim sat between us. Denny was a giant of a man of six feet four with the large hands of a ploughman. In contrast Jim was small, thin and wiry. All went well until after the communion when the priest turned round to preach his sermon. Seeing a number of soldiers in the body of the church he seemingly departed from his usual sermon and instead availed of the opportunity to welcome them as the saviours of our country. Before he could get any further into his oration Jim jumped up and in no uncertain terms protested saying he would not listen to this attempt to turn the mass and the church into a political platform. In turn Jim was quickly silenced by Denny who placed one of his hands over Brislane's mouth, pushed him back into his seat saying: "Sit down Jim Brislane and listen to the Word of God." Fortunately Jim's innate sense of humour came to the rescue and he burst out laughing. This was too much for the priest who turned abruptly back to the altar to conclude the mass.'

We later managed to fire the barracks and we left the town of Buttevant with the night sky reflecting the red glow of the burning building.

Without making much delay in Mallow we moved on to Dromahane where we set up a temporary head-quarters. Here I called a meeting of the available Divisional Staff and the local Battalion Officers, Ned Murphy, Tom Daly, Jerry O'Hanlon, Tadhg Byrnes, Mick O'Connell, Batt Walsh and Jerry Buckley. Although the overall picture was pretty grim these men were determined to continue a guerrilla fight. It was decided to blow up the Mallow Viaduct and so cut the Dublin—Cork railway route.

Before leaving this area around Lombardstown I could not help contrasting my present feelings with those I had when I first arrived there with Liam Lynch in July 1921 to set up the headquarters of the First Southern Division. Then we lived in an atmosphere of victory, rejoicing in the new found freedom of move-ment and the warm welcome from those good people who like ourselves in West Cork had lived through such hard and dangerous times. Here, too, we had renewed friendships with many visitors from the Fourth Cork Brigade and the Kerry Brigades which were now included in the Division. In one short year we had seen the collapse of our fondest hopes and our dreams of complete victory.

To give my personal recollections of what followed on our return from Dublin on 28 June is a very dif-ficult assignment after fifty years. There was for instance the mobilisation of our forces from Cork, Kerry and West Limerick to support Liam Lynch when he moved into Limerick in early July. Following on this we got a number of columns to re-inforce the line across Tipperary from Golden, Cashel to Carrick-on-Suir. Many of our units fought here, many officers and men were captured and we had fatal casualties. While Lynch was in Limerick I made many visits along the line and on one of them met de Valera in the Carrick-on-Suir area where he was acting as Adjutant in a Tipperary column in the Carrick-on-Suir district. Seamus Robinson was the O/C South Tipperary and subsequently became O/C Second Southern Division. There were many other prominent Volunteers in the area including Sean Fitzpatrick, Dan Breen, Sean Hogan, Ned O'Reilly, Mick Sheehan, Denny Lacey, Bill Quirke and Jimmy Leahy of Mid-Tipperary. At that time we were hopeful of being able to hold the Waterford-Limerick line intact as a bulwark to south Munster but this possibility was nullified by our opponents use of coast-wide shipping to land troops at strategic points.

After the occupation by the Free State troops of Waterford on 23 July, I spent two days in Dungarvan looking at the proposed defence of west Waterford. In theory it looked an excellent plan. It was mainly based on the defence of the Colligan river and we expected the added strength of a Column from the First Cork Brigade under Pat Murray and a smaller unit from the Third Cork Brigade under the well known leader at Crossbarry, Tommy Kelleher. Yet in spite of the excellence of these experienced officers and men their defence could not withstand the attack or prevent the Free State forces from taking Dungarvan and the rest of west Waterford. Gradually all our units were being forced to retire and soon all of Waterford and south Tipperary was occupied. It was particularly disappointing in the cases of Carrick-on-Suir and Clonmel where we had the most experienced officers and best armed men of the South Tipperary Brigade. The defence we put up was, to say the least, weak but let me hasten to add that not one area in Munster at that time could boast that their campaign was anything better.

Yet the news was not always so depressing. I recall a swift operation by a column under the command of Sean Moylan who went from Limerick to Waterford and on their journey they captured the Free State held barracks at Cahirconlish. We had a substantial victory also in the Kilmallock area where two West Cork columns, commanded respectively by Maurice Donegan and Dan Holland, forced Free State forces to retreat in disorder between Kilmallock and Bruree. There were other successes but unfortunately I am not clear on the details or the names of those involved.

One personal incident however remains very clear to me. It emphasises the laxity characteristic of our forces. While I was carrying out a late evening inspection of the Kilmallock line I came to an important cross-roads on the main Limerick— Charleville road. The defence of this cross-roads was vital to us since it could prevent an attack coming in from Limerick on our flank. I found only one man on duty there. He told me that six others had gone to Charleville for a drink. I found them drinking in the late Sean O'Briens bar. The only excuse or explanation they offered was that they were tired and weary of the long protective duty and had come to town for a bit of a break. All I could do was to order them to return back to their home unit and I then arranged for a more reliable replacement from our reserve force at Buttevant.

About this time I had a visit from Bill Ahern, a man I had known by reputation only as an active Volunteer in the London Brigade. He was a native of Mitchelstown and had emigrated to England in 1914 and by the time the truce came he was known, with Sam Maguire and Reggy Dunne, as one of the most active and successful officers in London. The services of these London men have not yet received the recognition and appreciation which is most certainly their due.

When the Civil War started Bill Ahern was still in London. Sam Maguire was tipped off that his identity had become known and he slipped quietly back to Dublin. Because of his great loyalty to Michael Collins, Sam joined the Treaty forces. Reggy Dunne was in Pentonville prison with his companion Joe Sullivan for the shooting of Sir Henry Wilson and both were eventually hanged on this charge. Ahern was therefore alone and had no real communication with Dublin. His leanings were with the anti-Treaty side and when he arrived in Ireland he immediately contacted Liam Lynch who advised him to come and see me at Buttevant. I felt, however, that Bill Ahern was very important in the movement across the water and I consequently advised him to return to London and there await developments. Being the fine Volunteer that he was he accepted this decision without question and left for London on the Fishguard boat from Cork that night. There he remained until 1940. I know that many Volunteers and their friends who either lived

71

there or passed through London, had reason to appreciate the help and advice of a man who had so many valuable contacts. His subsequent return to Ireland and his success as a business executive was entirely in keeping with his invaluable services in the enemy stronghold.

Any possibility of our forces mounting a full scale defence of Munster was by now discounted. The Free State forces were well organised and fully equipped with arms, artillery, armoured cars and transport. They had taken us by surprise when they began landing troops at strategic points on the coast. The first landing had been made at Waterford on 23 July. On 2 August a landing was made at Fenit pier and troops quickly occupied Tralee, Castleisland and Killarney without opposition. The greatest blow of all was the landing at Passage West on 8 August. This was unexpected and due to superior armour our forces retreated in disorder. When part of our force did eventually reach Ballincollig a further order was given to continue on to Macroom, but instead many of the men just returned to their homes. When Lynch heard of these landings he evacuated the two barracks in Fermoy and ordered them to be burned on 11 August.

This was really, for all of us, the bitter end of the first phase of the Civil War. The solid south, in which we had so much confidence, was completely broken. After the evacuation of Buttevant barracks the men of the Kerry Brigades returned to their own areas. The men of the Cork Brigades did likewise, and after the evacuation of Cork city there was a general exodus towards the mountainous districts of West Cork, principally to Donoughmore, Ballinagree, Coolea and Ballinageary. The policy we were now forced to adopt was a return to guerrilla warfare and despite all the reverses, we still hoped to repeat our successes of the Black and Tan War in this field.

Unfortunately we were forced to realise that things were not the same. Two major factors militated against the success of our new planning. The people were no longer enthusiastically with us as in the earlier fight. That had been for them a gruelling period of tension and persecution and they were unwilling to face a renewal of such conditions when there was an alternative of peace, even at a price. The second factor was the reluctance of so many Volunteers to face up to the harsh realities. They seemed to have no heart in the fight and the knowledge that they were fighting against their kith and kin, even brother against brother, must also have influenced them very much. The Divisional Staff and the senior officers tried to maintain morale and to rally them at various points even where there was no fighting, but it was becoming increasingly clear to me that a cessation of hostilities then would have been the better policy.

I knew at that time that this was the feeling of many senior officers, but Liam Lynch remained adamant and would not entertain any suggestion of seeking terms. He was to the very end an idealist with the highest principles as his guide and it was not in his nature to surrender or to compromise. He ultimately gave his life for those principles. I have always felt that his promise to support the Four Courts garrison if they were attacked remained a sacred trust and the two

73

broken treaties which he had signed in Limerick with Donncha O'Hannigan and Michael Brennan confirmed his determination that this would be a fight to the finish. On the other hand de Valera himself had no illusions and had stated that a military victory was not possible. In his own words he said: 'In fact after the burning of the barracks and the abandonment of territory without need and without any attempt to defend it in August 1922 I thought there was no hope of winning.' He continued to pursue his efforts towards peace. About this time a fresh effort was made by two prominent men who were prisoners in Kilmainham. On 24 August Tom Barry wrote on behalf of Oscar Traynor and himself to the Minister of Defence, Dick Mulcahy, asking for an interview 'on the matter of vital importance that concerns the future of the nation'. They were interviewed by Liam Tobin and they suggested that they should get permission to visit Mountjoy to see Rory O'Connor, Joe McKelvey and Liam Mellows to discuss with them how to bring about an ending of hostilities. This request was refused and no doubt the refusal was influenced by the death of Michael Collins a few days earlier. Again on 12 December, Sean T. O'Kelly and Oscar Traynor writing from Gormanston Internment Camp asked for parole so that they might discuss peace terms with their colleagues but were refused. And so the Civil War dragged on into the New Year.

After the landing of Free State troops at Passage West I made a few brief calls on friends in the Lombardstown area and I then set out for Cork to ascertain the exact position for myself. When I reached the outskirts of the city I heard the grim news of the evacuation and withdrawal to Macroom. I then travelled to West Cork and made my first visit to the Hyde house of Toureen. I had not been there since the famous ambush in October 1920. It was then occupied by a family named Roberts who sold it to the Hyde family, who were now in the forefront of the opposition to the Treaty. Sean was a recently qualified veterinery surgeon. When studying at University College, Dublin, he had won an All-Ireland Hurling medal with Dublin and was an active volunteer. He was now the Intellegence Officer on the Divisional Staff and was later appointed as O/C of the Western Command. In his enthusiasm he could not see defeat or perhaps, could not understand the meaning of the word. Later on I had reason to feel that his enthusiastic reports to Liam Lynch, at a time when our whole edifice seemed to be crumbling around us, did much to encourage and strengthen Liam in his determination to carry on the fight.

4. The Death of Collins

After an early breakfast on 21 August I left Hydes of Toureen and made a brief call to see my father and mother at Kilmacsimon. I then hurried on to Joe Sullivans at Gurranereagh, which had been one of my headquarters in the War of Independence and where I had already informed Liam Lynch I would now establish temporary headquarters for the Division. I received the same welcome as always from the Sullivan family though I did not know at the time that they were very much pro-Treaty.

Among the many dispatches waiting for me there was one from Liam Lynch who had then established his headquarters in the Fermoy-Glanworth area. This was to tell me that de Valera had been with him and was even then on his way to see me. Apparently Dev's mission was to try to bring the War to an end, but his suggestions and arguments would not be accepted in any way by Lynch who asked me not to give Dev any encouragement either. I worked through the day on the ordinary routine matters which needed attention and towards evening de Valera arrived.

We discussed the War situation far into the night. His main argument was that, having made our protest in arms and as we could not now hope to achieve a military success, the honourable course for us was to withdraw. Although agreeing in my heart with this argument I countered that we had at least one thousand men under arms in the First Southern Division and I felt sure that the majority of them would not agree to an unconditional cease fire.

Next morning, 22 August, we left Joe Sullivans and I conveyed de Valera to Béalnabláth Cross, about three miles away. We arrived there around 9.30 am. From there I had arranged that he would be conducted by Dinny Crowley to Ahadillane on his return journey to Liam Lynch in Glanworth. At the cross we were stopped by Denny Long who had been on scout duty during the night, because several Divisional Officers were billeted in Jerh Long's public house. He told us that a short time previously a Free State armed convoy consisting of a motor cyclist, a lorry of troops, a touring car and an armoured car had stopped to enquire the way to Bandon. Denny said he was most helpful to them as he was anxious to see them on their way quickly because of the Officers billeted in the nearby pub. He also told us that he recognised Michael Collins in the touring car. This was confirmed by Jerh Long who saw the convoy from his shop window. De Valera asked me what was likely to happen now and I replied that the men billeted in this area included many of those who had been forced to retreat from Limerick, Kilmallock and Buttevant and in their present frame of mind would consider this incursion into the area which was so predominantly Republican — in five company areas on this route to Bandon not one active volunteer had joined the Free State Army — as a challenge which they could not refuse to meet. I felt that an ambush would be prepared in case the convoy returned. De Valera then remarked that it would be a great pity if Collins were killed because he might be succeeded by a weaker man. De Valera then left us to rejoin Lynch in north Cork and was safely conducted to Glanworth.

In the company of Tom Crofts, Divisional Adjutant, I returned to Gurranereagh where we attended to many urgent matters and weighed up the new situation in which we found ourselves. I also sent a report on Dev's visit to Liam Lynch. In the meantime at Béalnabláth the Brigade Commandant, Tom Hales with a column of twenty-five men had taken up an ambush position about half a mile down the Bandon road. They were positioned on the western side of the road some fifteen to twenty yards behind a low fence on rising ground and a mine had been laid on the road.

That evening when we had completed the matters which needed attention, Crofts and I left Gurranereagh and walked the three miles to Béalnabláth arriving there at about 7 pm. Jerh Long told us that the column was in ambush position and I walked down the Bandon road in that direction. There I met Tom Hales who was standing in the middle of the road. He told me that as the men had been in such an uncomfortable position all day and as the convoy was not likely to return this way, he was giving an order to withdraw. He also ordered the Battalion Engineer to remove the mine and detailed four members of the column to remain in position as a protective party while this was being done. About twelve men of the column left in the direction of Newceston, while others, with Tom Hales and myself, walked back along the road to Béalnabláth Cross. After such a long, tiring day it was only natural that they should have a drink in Longs pub. We were in the pub about ten minutes when we heard the sound of machine-gun and rifle fire coming from the direction of the ambush position. We rushed out to a higher road, the old Béalnabláth-Bandon road, which ran parallel to the lower road. We crossed a few fields and then came in sight of the ambush position. We had come very quickly and it had not taken us more than fifteen minutes since hearing the first shots. From where we were, some three hundred yards from the actual position, we could see very little — just a lorry and the turret of the armoured car with a few soldiers darting from one position to another. We had fired a few shots when suddenly the whole convoy moved off. Later on we were joined by the covering party at the ambush site, who reported that as far as they knew, there were no casualties on either side although their position was under withering fire from the machine gun in the armoured car. Twilight had set in by now but the actual firing had taken place in day-light.

Six members of the column who laid the ambush were Brigade Officers and were in the area to attend a Brigade Council meeting that night at Murrays house. Here they were given a meal and waited for the others to begin the meeting. This meeting began at 9.30 pm attended by myself and the following officers: Tom Crofts, Divisional Adjutant, Con Lucey, Divisional Director of Medical Services, Sean Culhane, Divisional I/O, Tom Hales, Brigade Commandant, Jim Hurley, Brigade Commandant, Tadhg O'Sullivan, Brigade Commandant, John Jordan, Brigade Commandant, Pete Kearney, O/C Third Battalion, Tom

Kelleher, O/C Fifth Battalion, Sean Hyde, O/C Western Command, Dan Holland, O/C First Battalion, Mick Crowley, Brigade Engineer. We had barely started when Sean Galvin of Crookstown rushed in and excitedly told us that Michael Collins had been shot dead in the ambush and the convoy had taken his body to Cork via Crookstown, Cloughduv and Killeeny.

The meeting was adjourned immediately and many of us left Murrays with heavy hearts. To those of us who had known Michael Collins personally, and there were many, his death was tragic: to Tom Hales, Tadhg O'Sullivan and myself who had known him intimately, our sorrow was deep and lasting. We parted without discussion of any kind. Tom Crofts and I walked back to Gurranereagh, a silent journey, each of us all too conscious of the tragedy and the loneliness that only time would heal. Crofts was a great friend of Johnny Collins, Michael's elder brother, and this friendship had been further cemented when they were together as prisoners on Spike Island in 1921. This was a relationship that survived the Civil War.

A lot has been written about this ambush at Béalnabláth by Irishmen who dramatised the action out of all proportion. Strangers also did not help in what they wrote, many of whom caused much pain. One writer states that four anti-Treaty officers, including Sean Lehane and myself, stayed at Joe Sullivans the night before the ambush and that Sean Lehane returned the next day and boasted on arrival: 'We got your friend Mickeen'. This is simply not true. To all who knew Sean Lehane such an expression could never be attributed to him, and furthermore at that particular point in time he was directing operations in Donegal, nearly three hundred miles to the north.

The following day we sent a full report of the ambush to Liam Lynch and we then had time to reflect on what had led up to this tragic event. I found it hard to accept that the convoy was travelling merely on a social visit to West Cork. It is mere conjecture, but I rated it as the foolhardy act of a brave man who knew well the area he was driving through and the men there who had so successfully overcome the might of the British Army, the sinister aggressiveness of the RIC, the brutality of the Black and Tans, and the ferocity of the Auxiliaries. This may seem a harsh judgement, yet I offer it whilst maintaining the impression I formed of Michael Collins when I first met him fifty-six years ago. I considered him then to be the greatest leader of our generation and I have not since changed that opinion. This last expedition of his may have been the gesture of a man who felt that reconciliation was no longer possible with so many intimate friends and comrades in West Cork. His death caused nothing but the deepest sorrow and regret and brought about in many of us a real desire for the end of the war. As de Valera had predicted he was followed by men of lesser vision and understanding whose actions bred a festering sore that still remains.

Nobody knew better than Collins the area through which he would pass, and consequently he arranged to travel in full military convoy. As such there could be no question of any intention on his part, as was suggested elsewhere, of meeting us for discussions.

81

The men who were billeted in and around Béalna-bláth had only arrived there the previous day after an unsuccessful campaign throughout Munster. They were there to attend a Brigade Council meeting at which the possibility of ending the War was likely to be discussed.

When the news that the convoy had driven on to Bandon was conveyed to the Brigade Commandant his natural reaction was to organise an ambush. It was indeed an extraordinary thing that the convoy did return by the same route considering that there were four other roads by which it could have travelled safely to Cork. If the route had been planned by Emmet Dalton, then G.O.C. Free State Forces in Cork and in charge of the convoy, I could understand it as he was a Dublin city man and had not a very great knowledge of the south. But for Collins to have submitted to such an arrangement was inexplicable and in military terms — baffling. Similarly, when attacked by the covering party of four, Dalton is said to have ordered full speed ahead but Collins countermanded this order, the cars screamed to a halt and the fight was on. This lasted almost a half hour and the machine gunner, Jock McPeak, a Scot, literally tore the ditches in shreds with the fierce fusilade of bullets from his machine-gun. He was actually down to his last belt of ammunition when the gun jammed. He popped his head out of the turret for a quick look around and as he ducked back a bullet chipped the paint off the rim of the turret. The engagement ended as the convoy drove off and the attackers had no knowledge of any casualty.

5. Brother Against Brother

The Civil War had only begun when initiatives started to bring it to an end. These initiatives continued at different levels and by different parties, groups and even by individuals but in no case were they successful. One of these efforts was initiated by Emmet Dalton who occupied Cork city in August. Through intermediaries he made contact with some Republican officers and he was actively assisted by Tom Ennis, an old Dublin Brigade officer. These feelers had the authority of the Free State Government, but because they insisted on unconditional surrender they had no hope of any success. When I reported this to Liam Lynch on 6 September, he said that Dalton and Ennis were undoubtedly acting on government orders and he could not understand why they did not contact him directly. Nevertheless Tom Ennis and Charlie Russell continued to explore every avenue of approach and eventually a meeting was arranged near Crookstown on 13 October. Tom Barry, Sean Hyde and myself were given safe conduct passes and we drove to the house of Tadhg O'Donovan, who was at that time medical officer of the First Cork Brigade. Also present that night were Fr Tom Duggan and Dr Paddy Kiely who had also given his services to sick and wounded Volunteers.

When Tom Ennis and Charlie Russell arrived the meeting began and, at the outset, I stated that our Executive had disapproved of the previous meeting and had reluctantly agreed to the present one. I naturally added that the new legislation, then being put through the Dáil, angered our members so much that they had decided to meet this latest challenge by carrying out reprisals against all those responsible for the bill which established military courts and granted to them powers of execution for unauthorised possession of arms. Despite this unpleasant introduction the discussions that followed were conducted on a friendly basis and we parted on good terms. The proposals put forward at this meeting by Ennis and Russell were reported to the Executive at their meeting at Ballybacon a few days later. They were of such a nature they did not merit serious consideration.

After our meeting we were entertained to a substantial and welcome tea my Mrs O'Donovan after which Fr Duggan conveyed us to O'Connells of Ballingillee, near Kilumney, where we stayed overnight. Next morning we parted company with Sean Hyde. Barry and I continued to Coppeen where Tom Crofts and Sean Culhane were waiting for news of the week's proceeding.

Later Crofts and I had a long talk in which I told him of Liam Lynch's decision to create a new command for the area now covered by the First, Second and Third Divisions, the First Western which included Clare and South Galway, and the Third Eastern which was mainly County Wexford. This proposed new area would now include all Munster with the counties Offaly, Laois, Kilkenny and Wexford. I was to take over command of this whole area with Con Moloney acting as Command Adjutant. In addition I was also appointed Deputy Chief-of-Staff and I explained to Crofts that Lynch intended to complete this new scheme by the creation of two more commands: one west of the Shannon and the other north of the Boyne and finally, that he Crofts, was to take over command of the First Southern Division.

While neither of us was over enthusiastic about the new commands we both accepted them without question and were quite satisfied to continue serving under Liam Lynch's leadership. Although I did not always agree with Liam Lynch I have always felt that, if he had survived, our life-long friendship would not have been damaged. At this time many of us hoped that those in the Free State army who had been active Volunteers in the Black and Tan War would break away and return to their first allegiance. This hope was strengthened by the introduction of the Execution Bill in the Dáil which we believed must have been repugnant to so many of our old comrades in the Free State army. But that hope was not realised. Tom Crofts especially expressed the fear that this Bill would create a new wave of bitterness where, up to now, there was at least some hope of a mutual understanding. To both of us it seemed provocative and unnecessary. We were well and truly beaten long before this—in fact almost from 20 June when we had declared our support for the men in the Four Courts it was a losing battle. It was little more than a protest and we were at all times on the defensive and constantly retreating. After Limerick and the collapse of the Bruff-Kilmallock line there were only a few isolated pockets of resistance left.

When historians come to write this period of our history they will find that very few of the Republican leaders had any mind for the killing of former comrades and consequently did not encourage battles or even offensive tactics of any serious or worthwhile value. For my own part I cannot say that I saw it all as clearly in October 1922 as I do now and did my part in maintaining the resistance.

I spent the next few days with Tom Crofts at Divisional Headquarters at Coppeen discussing with him and few other officers all matters of importance and handing over to him all correspondence relating to the administration of the Division. In the course of the day a dispatch arrived from Erskine Childers informing us that he was returning to Dublin and would be contacting us at Coppeen that evening. Erskine, with his cousin David Robinson, had been editing *An Phoblacht* and assisting them were men whose names illuminated the literary world some years later. They included Sean O'Faolain, Frank O'Connor and Sean Hendrick. I sent for our most dependable dispatch rider Denny Crowley — the blacksmith's son from Castletownkenneigh — and on his recommendation I took Erskine and David to Jerh Longs house at Shanacashel not far from Kilmichael, scene of the famous ambush in November 1920. I knew that the Longs were a pro-Treaty family and, when asking for accommodation for the three of us I enquired it this request would cause them any embarrassment. Mrs Long gave us a very hearty welcome indeed and her hospitality was the best assurance of her goodwill towards us.

After a substantial meal we sat around a large turf fire with our host and some members of his family. Mrs Long joined us around 11 o'clock and told us that beds were now ready for the three of us. David Robinson gladly accepted the invitation but Erskine Childers was silent. After a little while I suggested he should retire in view of the long an hazardous journey ahead of him on the following day. He replied quietly but firmly that he would not accept a bed which would deprive some of the children of their night's rest. As he was quite adamant I went and told Mrs Long and assured her he would be quite comfortable sitting at the fire.

Erskine's cousin, David Robinson, was very active in the four months he spent with us in the south. He had been an officer in the British army and was inclined at times to contrast his Sandhurst training with our free and easy approach in guerrilla warfare. He rarely missed an opportunity of lecturing us on military discipline. Many stories are told about him and some are very amusing as, for instance, when he appeared in the attack that led to the re-capture of Kenmare carrying no arms but a walking stick which caused a supporter to remark to John Joe Rice 'I thought ye were serious up till now.' On another occasion in the planning of a surprise attack on Inchigeela barracks he seriously suggested the borrowing of a baby from one of the intinerant families in the neighbourhood and volunteered to take the baby to the door of the barracks appealing for alms in the hope of its being opened. Needless to say the experienced Battalion Commandant, Paddy O'Sullivan did not accept the suggestion.

In 1924 Dr Dorothy Stopford Price, who had been such a sterling friend to us in the Black and Tan War, and who was a close friend of the Barton family, sent an invitation to Tadhg O'Sullivan, Seán Buckley and myself to visit Annamoe in Co. Wicklow as guests of Robert Barton. Here we renewed our acquaintance with David Robinson who was then living there and, as a result, I think we came to understand him better, and to appreciate his point of view.

After breakfast in Longs Denny Crowley arrived with a horse and trap and set out with our guests for Ahidillane, some thirty miles to the north east. As I bade good-bye to Childers that morning I did not imagine it was a final one. He arrived at Annamoe, the home of his cousin Robert Barton, four days later. He was captured there that night and a week later was executed in Beggar's Bush Barracks in Dublin.

When I completed handing over my command at Coppeen I set out for my new post and after three days foot-slogging over some eighty miles, I arrived at Mrs Tobins of Tincurry on the main Cork–Dublin road some three miles beyond Mitchelstown. The new command was to set up headquarters somewhere near here with Tobins the centre and call house. Con Moloney was already in possession and had occupied the neighbouring house of the Butlers.

Two days later we attended a meeting of the Second Division at Mahers of Black Castle in the Rosegreen district. After the meeting Con returned to Tincurry and I set out for north Tipperary with Jimmy Leahy, O/C Mid-Tipperary as my guide. It was a day of much

Free State activity around Rosegreen, Cashel and Thurles and we had to make our way cross country, avoiding main and secondary roads. It was a tiring day in late November although the brilliant sunshine was most unusual for the time of year. We reached Boher-lahan at dusk only to be surprised by two lorries full of troops. We were lucky that they did not see us as we vaulted the wall opposite the church. When the lorries left we continued our journey and reached the Leahy house at Tubberadora, beyond Boherlahan, just as the senior member of the family, Johnny, arrived in from Thurles. It was Sunday and he had been attend-ing a GAA meeting there. Though an active Volunteer in the Black and Tan War, Johnny was now neutral and he was therefore free to travel and meet whom he wished. After the meeting in Thurles Johnny met Jerry Ryan of Moycarkey who was the O/C of the Free State forces in Mid-Tipperary with headquarters in Templemore. Jerry had been active in the War of Independence and he too felt at the time that some-thing should be done to bring the unfortunate conflict to an end, before any further executions would sever old friendships and breed lasting bitterness.

I left Tubberadora with Jimmy and set out for Kil-common. We took a short cut and by-passed Holy-cross and somewhere between Drombane and Upper-church we turned in to an avenue which led to a large house. It was close to midnight when we knocked and were welcomed by a man whose accent and general appearance marked him as a retired Englishman. When he saw us he opened the door saying: 'Gentle-men, I do not know who you are, neither do I want to know but you are both welcome to the hospitality of my house.' This welcome was genuine: we were given a meal and had a good night's rest there. When we left the next morning he wished us well. Without further difficulty we eventually reached Kilcommon Cross and the home of Pakey Ryan one of the best known hosts in all Tipperary. After a week in this wonderful part of the country I experienced and fully appreciated the warm hospitality about which Charles Kickham had so eloquently written in his novels.

I had been continously on the run for almost two weeks after leaving Coppeen and had covered one hundred and forty miles on foot. I slept soundly at night and quite often late in to the morning, and I was given every help and comfort by these gracious, kindly Tipperary people. Pakey Ryan's contacts were legion and he soon had me in touch with Paddy Ryan Lacken, who was then the O/C North Tipperary in succession to Sean Gaynor and Paddy MacDonnell, both of whom had been captured. When reporting the present position Lacken told me of a meeting of the Third Southern Division which was to be held at Powells of Ballynaclough in the Toomevara district two days later. He had made arrangments for transport to cover the twelve miles. This was most welcome news as I was then developing a chest cold which was to plague me for the next six weeks.

At this point of time the Third Southern Division included north Tipperary and practically all of Offaly and Laois, two counties with which I had no previous contact. Consequently I was very anxious to ascertain the actual position in both. Lacken and I discussed this at length, as well as the adjoining areas of East and Mid-Limerick. Because so many officers were in jail north Tipperary was considered dormant, with the exception of the district from Rear Cross in the west to Kilcommon north of Templederry, areas which included the north Tipperary mountains. Here with a very small force, we were more than holding our own in keeping the Free State forces at bay. The area from Nenagh to the Offaly border was fully in their hands and there was nothing we could do about it. The same depressing situation applied to East and Mid-Limerick, with the exception of a small area around Castleconnell where Sean O'Carroll — a prominent County Limerick hurler in his day — was remarkably active with his small unit although he was hemmed in on all sides.

This news of course was not very surprising as the vast majority of those who had fought so successfully in the War of Independence were now serving under their leader, Donncha O'Hannigan, and their example encouraged large numbers of new recruits. I could only recall a few of the pre-Truce leaders who were serving on our side. These included Tom Malone, Dave Clancy (of Cush), and the Clancy brothers of Ballylanders. This was not a very encouraging picture but somehow Paddy Ryan Lacken could always look on the bright side of things probably hoping for the miracle that never happened.

The following night we set off in a back-to-back pony trap for Toomevara. I sat in front with the driver, Jim Murphy, while Paddy Lacken with Paddy Hughes, an outstanding Volunteer of which I was to see a great deal in our later captivity, sat behind. It was a clear, bright night as we approached a crossroads about three miles east of the Silvermines. It seemed as if Jim suddenly propelled himself from his seat and disappeared behind the fence on the right hand side of the road. I grabbed the reins and pulled up the pony. From the rear Lacken shouted, 'Where is that so and so gone to?' We got down to investigate and as we did so Jim's head appeared over the fence with the apologetic explanation, 'I don't know what came over me but I could have sworn the cross roads was full of soldiers.' 'Bloody well asleep and dreaming you were,' replied Lacken. After some more banter we continued on our way in the direction of Toomevara.

Eventually, without further incident, we reached Powells of Ballynaclough, a very friendly Protestant family, where we received once again a typical Tipperary welcome. We remained there for two days and two nights but the expected officers from Offaly and Laois failed to turn up or send any communication to us. We wondered what had happened and finally came to the conclusion that they had been captured on their way. Normally this disappointment would have shaken my confidence in what I was doing but in the very difficult circumstances in which we were living at the time I accepted the position as it was and with my three companions I faced back from the plains of Toomevara to the comparative safety of the Tipperary hills.

On the return journey my chest trouble had developed and I felt I was in for a serious bout of illness. In this emergency Lacken took over and decided we would carry on to Rear Cross and then to a house of a friend of his on the southern slopes of Slieve Felim. An unusual feature of this high ground was that it was occasionally enveloped in a thick fog which made travel there impossible and thus added to its security.

It was then 4 December and I can never forget the kindness of the lady of the house who cared for me with all the skill of a trained nurse. On the evening of 7 December the area was free of fog and Lacken arrived with a copy of the daily paper which carried the startling news that two Dáil deputies had been attacked in Dublin. Sean Hales was dead and Padraig Ó Maille was wounded. On the following morning four Republican prisoners, Rory O'Connor, Liam Mellows, Joe McKelvey and Dick Barrett were taken from their cells in Mountjoy and executed by firing squad. All four were personal friends of mine, although I differed with Rory on his methods as a member of the Executive. The tragic news of those two days fairly shattered me. With my physical condition at such a low ebb and being so much on my own I passed through a period of the greatest depression. For twenty-four hours I could think of nothing but the shooting of Sean Hales and that at the hands of my comrades. This was something for which I felt a personal responsibility as a member of the Executive that had made the order in October. The reprisals completed the tragedy and brought home the desperation and savage hate caused by this Civil War. Sean Hales and Dick Barrett, two of my most intimate and personal friends were now dead and for what? In that quiet, lonely house on the mountain-side memories of many years came flooding back.

Sean, who was twelve years my senior, was a close and dear friend. In the beginning of the century he had organised a hurling club and was also one of the poineers of the Volunteer movement. His brother Tom was the first O/C of the Third Cork Brigade and when it was formed in January 1919, Sean was appointed Commandant of the First Battalion (Bandon) and I was his Adjutant. Both brothers served terms of imprisonment in British jails. Then came the terrible Civil War and Sean became O/C of the Free State troops in Bandon. He held that post when Michael Collins paid his last visit there and his brother Tom was the O/C who had mounted the ambush at Béalnabláth. This was the tragic story of several families torn apart by the Civil War.

Dick Barrett I had known since I first played against him in a football match in 1917. He was then a school-teacher and deeply involved in all things national. During the period 1920-1921 our relationship became much more intimate as we fought side by side in the ranks of Volunteers. He eventually became the Brigade Quartermaster, and was arrested in February 1921. Shortly after his release he was again taken into captivity after Crossbarry and moved to Spike Island. Here he remained until November 1921 when with five others he made a spectacular escape. He was later promoted to the staff of the First Southern Division. He joined Rory O'Connor in the Four Courts and it was there he was taken prisoner. Now he was dead, and the future seemed to me to hold no promise of any respite in the grim litany of disasters.

Through a sleepless night I tried to analyse the reason, cause or purpose, of what was happening and not unnaturally I attributed it all to the Treaty. I recalled a meeting of th IRB in Parnell Place, Cork in the previous November. It was a large gathering including practically every centre of south Munster — Cork, Kerry, Waterford, West Limerick. Before going into the meeting Michael Collins had a private talk with Liam Lynch, Florrie O'Donoghue and myself — we were respectively Divisional Centre, Cork County Centre and Divisional Secretary. Before the meeting Collins said privately but quite definitely that there would have to be some compromise in the current negotiations in London. There was no question of our getting all the demands we were making. Lynch asked Collins not to repeat this at the meeting or else it would 'blow up'. Collins made no reply and we went into the meeting. He was enthusiastically welcomed by the delegates and it was a harmonious session. No difficult questions were introduced and it ended with the usual exchanges of friendship between Collins and the many delegates.

Thinking back on that meeting I wondered if Lynch was wrong in stopping Collins from issuing a warning that a Republic was not on the cards? I thought he was and felt it would have been better if Collins had ignored Lynch and put his cards on the table rather than encouraging his audience in the hope that the promised land was round the corner. At that meeting he was among friends, tried and true, and I felt they should have been put fully in the picture. As I lay there on my sick bed I saw clearly the terrible weaknessess that dogged our side. We had no real military policy. No discussion ever took place on the strategy and tactics we should adopt in the event of the Provisional Government forcing us to fight a Civil War. I saw clearly the futility of some commanders from the country areas electing to fight in the Four Courts instead of in their own country areas. At best the Four Courts could only be considered as a protest in arms with failure as the inevitable end. Perhaps these thoughts were the result of illness and loneliness in that house on the slopes of Slieve Felim. I had no feelings of anger against my colleagues of the Executive. It had become clearly evident to me that we were not prepared for this war which should have ended with the fall of the Four Courts. As the war went on we were driven underground and the most distressing feature of all was the ever increasing knowledge that we had lost the support of the people. In the War of Independence their hospitality, their generosity and their bravery were the real backbone of the struggle. True we were still given food and shelter but I could not help feeling that for the most part we were being tolerated because of who we were or because of our success in earlier times.

It was here that I differed with Liam Lynch, who saw a future hope of victory where I saw none. Liam at his headquarters depended a lot on written reports, many of which were grossly exaggerated and highly misleading. But a few however told him the truth. Con Moloney, writing to him from the Glen of Aherlow on 4 December did not encourage him to think that a military victory was possible. The army, Con said, faced a virtual stone wall. Local initiative was dead and there was a growing danger of a breakdown in discipline.

I recalled that when I reached Glanworth on my way to an executive meeting at Goaten Bridge in October 1922 I could not contact a single Volunteer to guide us over the Kilworth mountains to Araglin. We managed to pick up a local individual but he lost his way in the darkness of the night, and we were fortunate indeed to meet another more dependable guide who led us safely away from the enemy camp and the occupied village of Kilworth. It was much the same story on our return journey when we had to fight our way through a patrol in Castletownroche. It appeared to me then that no real resistance was being offered to the Free State Army, apart from the Second Kerry and Fifth Cork Brigades and that we could never achieve anything we hoped for. Despite all this Lynch was entirely unmoved in his steady determination to continue the fight. He issued a circular on *Peace Moves* in which he stated: 'No terms short of independence can be accepted by the Army or Government'. If only Lynch had travelled through his area a little more and consulted with his officers on the spot it just might have had some influence on his thinking. He was however, so set on victory that I doubt even this would have changed his thinking.

Time passed very slowly during my illness and on the 14 December I got out of bed when Paddy Lacken called and I made arrangements with him to leave the next day. Later that night when undressing for bed I discovered a new and very unpleasant development. I saw the first signs of the dreaded scabies appear on my thighs. This was a common infection which many of us had experienced two years earlier. It followed the annoying itch which was attributed to the thinning or a weakening of the blood. Next morning the disease had spread further and I realised that I would have to see a doctor immediately.

Having called at Kilcommon Cross to bid good-bye to Packey Ryan I spent the night at a point nearer to Hollyford — Ryans of Filedarrig. The next morning I was covered with broken skin from hips to toes, with blood and matter oozing from the skin breaks; Lacken, who had remained with me suggested a visit to a Dr McCormack at Oola. This doctor lived on our road, close to the Cross of Cluggin. Fortunately the doctor was at home and he treated and bandaged the affected parts. He also helped me to cross the danger point on the Limerick to Limerick Junction road, by driving me in his pony and trap to Lattin, a village close to Emly.

At about nine o'clock we entered Lattin and there I saw Jerry Kiely of Tipperary town and Dan Breen. With a deep sense of gratitude I bade good-bye to Dr McCormack and drove in another horse and trap with Breen and Kiely on to Rossadrohid where we spent the night at the alternative Command Headquarters at Tincurry. The following day, with much difficulty and much pain, I crossed the Galtees to Butlers where I had to remain in bed for three weeks. Fortunately for me a member of the family, Chris, who later married Sean Hogan, was a trained nurse and, under the direction of Dr John Stokes of Cahir, gave me unremitting attention. Because of the nature and extent of the complaint my whole body needed bandaging, which was a painful and most unpleasant experience. It is some little satisfaction for me now to place on record how much I owed to those good friends whose kindness and professional services were so generously given.

Con Moloney visited me frequently and on Christmas Day 1922 he told me of a meeting with Seán Lehane, now O/C of the Eastern Division in Co. Wexford. Seán had been the Commandant of the Schull Battalion–one of the most successful in the West Cork Brigade. In the spring of 1922 he was sent by Liam Lynch to Donegal as the O/C of the First Northern Division in an effort to build up our forces on the Border. This however failed and he was now trying to revitalise Wexford. In a subsequent visit Con told me he had arranged for a meeting in mid-January with Sean Lehane at Walshs of Clogga, in the parish of Mooncoin. Among the visitors to the Butlers were Dan Breen, Bill Quirke and Sean Hogan who spent much time with me in my bedroom discussing current events.

Sean was then in charge of a column along the south-east Tipperary border. He was one of the most forthright colleagues whose courage and daring, beginning at Soloheadbeg in January 1919 and continuing to the ambush on Lord French at Ashtown, helped make a name for him in the War of Independence. He was not only a man of physical bravery but also of

strong moral courage. It was no surprise to me therefore, when we were alone one evening that he put the
direct question to me: 'When are ye going to call off
this useless war?' I thought to temporise but knowing
the seriousness of the question I told him in strict confidence of my own thinking and of my hopes of going
back to discuss the matter with the First Division Staff
and Brigade Officers. I had no direct knowledge of
their feelings, but in the previous August had been
told that a motion was to come before the Third
Brigade Council advocating withdrawal. It was to
have been sponsored by Jim Hurley, Tom Hales,
Tadhg O'Sullivan and Flor Begley. Unfortunately the
tragedy of Béalnabláth caused that meeting to be cancelled. I told Sean that I would go to Cork and discuss
the whole question with the various officers before
approaching Liam Lynch. Many years later when
Sean was living in Chapelizod he sent me a type-writ-
ten copy of his own memoirs and in it I found a full
account of this conversation and of his efforts on my
behalf after my capture.

On 6 January, when I was feeling somewhat better,
Bill Quirke and I set off for south Kilkenny to meet
Sean Lehane. I was very glad to have Bill as my companion for the O/C of the Second Southern Division
had been dogged with ill health and Bill stood out as
his natural successor. It was also imperative that he
should meet Lehane who was now commanding the
adjoining division. No one had a better knowledge of
the countryside than Quirke. He was the perfect
guide.

I should say in passing that in December 1922 a

force led by Bill and Tom Barry, and with a few selected leaders from the Cork Brigades, organised attacks on the Free State forces in Callan, Mullinavat, Thomastown and Carrick-on-Suir where heavy opposition was overcome. Large quantities of rifles, machine-guns, stores and clothing were taken from the four posts and although seven more Republicans had been executed that day we released all our prisoners.

The journey on which we now set out was some 60-70 miles through an area frequently patrolled by troops from Clonmel, Waterford and Kilkenny. Consequently most of the travelling had to be done by foot and at night. It was soon all too clear to us that the majority of the people we met were pro-Treaty but Bill Quirke's great personality overcame this and the hospitality extended to us was really extraordinary.

On the second night out from Tincurry when we were a few miles from Callan we were delayed some hours by three lorries from the Fethard district. This necessitated a change of direction which unfortunately added extra miles to our journey. Shortly after midnight Bill said we would bed down for the night and get some food. He rapped on the door of a fine looking house standing alone. After a pause a window was raised upstairs and a voice called out: 'What do you want?' to which Bill replied in a disguised voice, 'We want a bed.' 'We haven't a single vacant bed in the house.' Still in his disguised voice Bill shot back, 'Yearra, what are you talking about, man. There are two of us here and 'tis a double bed we want. Come down quick and open the door. We are famished.'

The order was obeyed, the door opened, an elderly man stood there holding a candle. Bill moved back leaving me in the candlelight for inspection. For a moment or so all was silent. Then Bill returned to the candlelight and with outstretched hands came the words: 'How are you, Mr Fennelly?' Consternation on the part of the host-to-be and the quick reply, 'You. . . You . . . should not have played this trick on me. Didn't you know well you are welcome into this house at any hour of the day or night.' He quickly ushered us into the sitting room and set a most attractive selection of bottles on the table before us. His lavish hospitality was even more evident the next day when we rose late after a very comfortable night's rest. At a lunch, more typical of Christmas day than the 8 January, we met the family. Well refreshed we set out on our journey. Mr Fennelly wished us God speed and added some advice suggesting that we stop the foolishness of our present campaign. Despite this admonition his parting words were: 'Bill, remember that you and your good friends are always welcome but for God's sake will you say who you are and don't be scaring me in the darkness of the night.'

In later years Bill spoke of two subsequent visits he paid to that house. The first was with Sean Hayes of Drangan and his second companion was Tom Bellews — a native of Dundalk who worked as a tin-smith mechanic in Cleeve's factory in Tipperary. In answer to the usual question 'Who is your friend?' Bill would have his joke and quite seriously say, 'This is Tom Bellews, a tinker from Dundalk.' This was surely a bit of a shock to Mr Fennelly but nevertheless Tom got his bed an the next day when the thaw set in and Tom's real profession was established he was treated as an honoured guest. As a companion in distress Bill Quirke had few equals, chiefly because of that enduring quality of optimism with which he faced every crises and his cheerful disposition which enabled him to laugh his way through the darkest hour.

Leaving Fennellys we travelled across the country to Grangemockler eight miles away. This area is best remembered perhaps on account of their footballers who were County Champions and as such were chosen to play Dublin at Croke Park on that infamous Bloody Sunday in 1920. As we came near the village I expressed a wish to call on Mrs Hogan, whose son Michael had been the goal keeper that day. He had been shot dead on the field, and his memory is perpetuated for all time by the Hogan Stand in Croke Park. We were given a hearty welcome by Mrs Hogan although her other son, Dan, was O/C of the Free State Northern Command. We continued on towards Mooncoin and stayed overnight at a friendly house near Kilmoganny.

On the journey we became painfully aware that because so many of our men had been captured the area had been left in a very weak organisational position and without local assistance we had to be extra careful. Eventually, twenty-four hours later we reached a house at the northern end of the parish and there we met Ted Moore, one of the most active officers now left in that district. He knew of our visit and the reason for it. He was actually on the look-out for our arrival in order to warn and save us from walking into a trap.

On the previous day, the day set for our meeting with Sean Lehane at Walshs of Clogga, the district was invaded by hundreds of Free State troops and Walshs was surrounded. No one escaped from the ring except Tom Bellews, who being trapped in a cow byre with the exits covered, managed to break a partition in the gable wall and get away under fire. We asked one another why was there enemy action on that particular day but there was no explanation. It seemed to us that information of our meeting had been leaked, or had accidently reached the Free State people many days beforehand, as this big show of strength could not have been arranged overnight. Some days later we learned the full facts. A few days previously Sean Lehane's headquarters in Wexford had been raided and he, together with his staff, dispatches and documents were taken. Bill Quirke and I were just fortunate to escape a trap well and carefully laid for us. Ted Moore was able to tell us that troops were still in occupation of Walshs house and were holding the roads leading to and from it. There was no choice therefore but to get out of the district.

To plan a route of retirement was not easy as we had no intimate knowledge of the country, and whatever route was chosen we would be very much on our own. Ted Moore mapped out a route that he considered safe. It led through the Bessborough Demense to a point at the Waterford side of Fiddown Bridge which was then held by Free State troops. There we hoped to find a friendly fisherman who would row us over the river to the Portlaw district on the Waterford side of the Suir. Having entered the demense we had to exercise great caution as it was certainly enemy territory. It was a bright moonlit night and we had to hug the fence closely. Eventually, we reached the main Waterford—Carrick-on-Suir road where before leaving us Ted found a local fisherman who volunteered to put us across the river which is tidal and was then at low water mark. The channel was narrow and the crossing was only a matter of minutes, but the boat was a small punt capable of taking only two people, so two trips were necessary. The boatman took me on the first crossing and landed me on fairly solid ground. This must have made me careless for suddenly, I stepped into a dreaded mud-hole. I say 'dreaded', because in my youthful years on the Bandon river I had stepped into a mud-hole, created by the lifting of slob mixed with seaweed, which was used as a fertiliser, and although the hole was only two feet deep, the incident was unpleasant. Here near Fiddown the situation was entirely different and presented a more serious problem. From the moment I stepped into that mud-hole I felt myself being slowly sucked down with no sign of a firm foothold. I nearly panicked at the thought of dying a slow, torturous death, but fortunately, managed to keep my head and stretched out my arms in an effort to check the suction. Although this was partially successful I was still sinking inch by inch and when the mud was up to my hips I had little hope. At that moment my feet felt a slight firmness and my arms were also finding some support. Gradually I levered myself up and somehow managed to drag myself out to firm land.

As I reached the river bank and safety, the punt

arrived. I shouted a warning to Bill. In the moonlight he picked his way carefully and when he saw the condition I was in he expressed his sympathy in one of his hearty laughs. We struck out for Clonea and for another of his many contacts. It was after midnight when we arrived at the home of his friends, the Stokes. The door was opened to our first knock and soon the whole family joined us, and although they had to smile at my bedraggled appearance they quickly make arrangements to remedy it. After a buffet meal I went to bed and my clothes were collected. We slept late the next day, and what a joy it was to find my suit washed, dried and pressed. No firm of cleaners could have done a better job. So comfortable were we that we needed little pressing to spend another night there.

The following day we set out for the Nire Valley in the Ballymacarbery district of west Waterford. Daily it was becoming more evident that Free State troops were patrolling the main roads, and on our first stage to Rathgormack we were warned that troops from Carrick-on-Suir were active. On the way I discussed with Bill the weak organisation that existed in this area and, although he agreed, he was still optimistic as long as Ted Moore was in charge. All in all, I felt that Kilkenny and Waterford could not be considered as likely to play any further active role in the fight.

Late at night we reached Rathgormack and Quirke led me to the home of another friend of his, Geoffrey Greene, a very strong pro-Treaty man and the leader of a new farmers' organisation, which was presently involved in a strike with farmers' labourers. This sub-

ject was strongly debated by Bill who favoured the
workers. While Greene had to admit the evils of the
strike he countered with the foolishness of our policy
and the ruin it was bringing on the country. This
debate or argument however did not effect the hospitality and Bill's unfailing good humour helped to end
the night on a pleasant note. Before retiring Bill
mentioned that we were heading for the Nire Valley
and transport was arranged there and then for the
following night. This was a welcome alternative to
another ten miles on foot.

When we were leaving our driver warned that the
danger spot was around Harpers Cross which was held
by troops from Clonmel, but our journey passed without incident and we reached O'Ryans in the Ballymacarbery district. This was one of the best known
homes in Tipperary during the War of Independence
and had continued throughout the Civil War and for
long afterwards. The Nire Valley, like the north Tipperary mountains was considered a reasonably safe
retreat for those on active service and reminded me of
similar areas in West Cork. We spent two happy
nights in this truly Republican homestead and then set
off on foot on the last stage of our journey to Tincurry
via Newcastle and Goaten Bridge.

In the short time that had elapsed since leaving,
enemy activity was evident everywhere in the area.
Troops from Cahir had been active and many houses
had been raided. From the nature of these raids it
looked as if they were now aware of the importance of
the area, probably from captured dispatches which
would have identified the existence of Command

headquarters in Tincurry.

Bearing all this in mind we decided to separate; I went to a house on the hillside up the Galtees to a family named O'Brien. Weary from the cross country journeys of the week I slept soundly until roused next morning by the owner with the news that the house was surrounded and soldiers were actually in the kitchen. I took a few seconds to realise where I was, and what had been said to me. As I became fully awake I saw an officer standing at the foot of the bed with a revolver. I was trapped, well and truly, with no option but to accept the position as it was. The officer was joined by others and they waited while I dressed. Then they searched the room and found a loaded revolver under the pillow and some extra rounds of ·45 ammunition in my trousers pocket. No word had been spoken but they waited until I had a cup of tea and a slice of bread. Then before leaving the house the officer, a Lieutenant Pollard from Killenaule, asked for my name, and on the spur of the moment I gave it as,'John Hurley, Ahidillane, Mallow'. Why this name I did not know then or even now. The loaded revolver was sufficient evidence for a charge and a name from Ahidillane (50 miles away) was bound to arouse suspicion even if no revolver or ammunition existed. Subsequently, I corrected the name, but as for as I now recall John Hurley remained on the charge sheet which was given to me before my trial in Clonmel.

6. The End of the Road

After I had been taken into custody we moved away from O'Briens and along the main Mitchelstown—Cahir road where we were joined by more units of the Free State troops who were evidently raiding houses in the Nire Valley. I cannot recall seeing any other prisoners, but my first feelings were of relief and delight that Bill Quirke had slept outside of this net and so escaped capture.

We marched to Cahir where I was locked in a room in a house adjoining Cahir House Hotel, which was then the Free State Headquarters. Here I spent the day in solitary confinement. The following day I was moved under escort to the Borstal School in Clonmel. My first visitor introduced himself as Ned McGrath, who was the O/C in the Cahir area. Actually he had been in charge of the operation in which I had been taken and also of the escort that had conveyed me from Cahir to Clonmel. He seemed surprised when I said I was glad to meet him, but only a short time previously Sean Hogan had mentioned two former prominent Volunteers who had good records but were now officers in the Free State Army, one was Ned McGrath, an active Captain of Skeheenarinkey Company which covered a large area on both sides of the Cahir—Mitchelstown road and including Kilbehenny in the east Limerick district. We talked freely and as he left he assured me he would do everything possible for me. I appreciated this gesture and thanked him, although at this stage I knew well what my fate would be. Incidentally, the second Volunteer that Hogan had mentioned was Tommy Ryan of Castlegrace, Clogheen who had been an active member of Hogan's column.

Later in the day another officer, Larry Joy from the Cappawhite-Annacarthy area, came to see me and told me he would be defending me at my court martial. I had also heard of Larry before and believed him to be a very sincere man. When he asked if there was any way in which I could help him with special considerations which might be useful in my defence I answered him with a broad smile. This he correctly interpreted and did not pursue the matter further. For the remainder of his visit we discussed in a friendly fashion the pre-Truce period and mutually regretted the unfortunate split and what it had brought to the country. Apart from these two, the orderly officer looked in a few times to assure himself, I suppose, that I was still safe in his custody. He was quite considerate in his visits and regularly enquired if I had any complaints about the way I was being treated. I had no complaints whatever and here I would like to take the opportunity of placing it on record that the treatment meted out to me while an officer prisoner in Clonmel, and subsequently for five weeks in Arbour Hill, was always such as I would expect from former Volunteers and comrades.

I have but a hazy recollection of what actually took place at the court martial on the following day the 20 January. Very little was said apart from the reading of the charges by the prosecuting officer who asked for the maximum penalty. I remained silent. The findings were apparently transmitted immediately by the special wireless telephone system used by army units to maintain communication with their headquarters in Dublin. A few hours later the sentence of the court was confirmed by GHQ and was relayed to the officer in command of the whole area, Major General T. Prout. It stated briefly that the sentence of death was to be carried out the following morning. Immediately after the news was conveyed to me I was asked if I had any reply, and I requested a stay of execution to enable me to get in touch with my fellow members of the Volunteer Executive with a view to urging the calling off of the war. This was relayed to Dublin and the reply came back very quickly.

As I recall it now, it simply stated that a stay of execution would only be granted on my signing an unconditional surrender. I would be given time to consider this but my reply must be yes or no. Faced with this ultimatum I sat down to consider my responsibility. If I were to agree there might be some hope of ending the war. If not then I had to face that I was leaving behind me a terrible mess for which I had much responsibility, as well as taking with me a very worried conscience on the rights and wrongs of our continuing the War. Were it a straight showdown of War between two armies on which I was definitely on the losing side I could not and would not interfere. For quite a long time the issue was not nearly as clear cut as that. It was evident to me, particularly after Limerick, that a victory on the field was definitely out. This view of mine was shared by many of our fighting

111

men, but we were soldiers and we felt our duty was to continue to obey orders.

The tactics of the Free State Government of reprisals had developed to such an extent that if allowed to continue would leave a legacy which would take generations to heal. These tactics had begun with the execution of Erskine Childers on the 24 November, although he claimed in his defence that he was an officer of the Republican Army. On 17 November four Volunteers were executed in Dublin. Major General Sean Hales was then shot in Dublin on the 7 December. The day after, 8 December, there followed such an act of savagery that it seemed all principles of war were abandoned. Four leaders, Rory O'Connor, Joe McKelvey, Liam Mellows and Dick Barrett were taken from their cells in Mountjoy and executed. Between 17 November and 31 January fifty-five Volunteers were executed in captivity. In addition many more in various parts of the country had been shot indiscriminately and counter reprisals only added further fuel to the fire. What followed the explosion of a trigger mine at Knocknagoshel was surely the lowest depths to which any established government or army could sink. At the dead hour of night nine men were taken from captivity in Tralee, five from Killarney and five from Cahirciveen, and were blown up by mines in addition to being shot at and having grenades thrown at them. Unbelievably two of the prisoners escaped. Stephen Fuller from Tralee and Tadhg Coffey from Killarney.

Here in the Borstal School in Clonmel I could review that whole position, and I saw the mistakes in leadership including my own. For me it had all begun with the truce on 11 July 1921, continuing with the signing of the Treaty, and culminating in the fatal Dáil debate followed by banning the Volunteer Convention in March 1922. From there on events had marched rapidly and, as I have already described, my responsibility weighed heavily on me. I write this now not as an excuse, but rather from the conviction that if it were in my power at that hour it was my duty to recommend a cessation of hostilities. As far back as August 1922 when de Valera, having seen Liam Lynch, had come to see me in West Cork about the possibility of ending hostilities, I had then felt that this would have been the right policy and during the intervening months I became more and more convinced of this view. In the south of Ireland where I had an intimate and personal knowledge of the great majority of those who were taking an active part in the anti-Treaty side there was no enthusiasm for this war. At most we could only say that we were protesting in arms. The tragedy was that our protest did not end with the fall of the Four Courts.

At this stage of my reflections Fr Keogh the chaplain arrived. He heard my confession and in a very touching way tried to console me. As he was leaving he said he would return again in the morning and bring me Holy Communion. Although I did not comment then, the hearing of my confession without asking any assurances in accordance with the Bishops' Pastoral surprised me, but it was also a source of much consolation. Another visitor was Lieutenant Hegarty whose feelings so over-came him that he broke down and cried. He had all my sympathy and I advised him to try and forget about it.When he left and I thought over his kind act in visiting me, I became more and more aware of the tragedy engulfing us all through our own fault. Lieutenant Hegarty was typical of his many colleagues in the Free State Army. They were caught up in the military discipline which was forcing them to carry out orders abhorrent to them.

As the night advanced I wrote some letters, two of them remain in my memory. One was to my mother, the other to Dan Breen. If any of the others are still extant which I doubt, they would reveal the state of my mind and my thinking on what might have been my last night on earth. The letters were handed to Colonel Prout and I was assured that they would be delivered as addressed.

Approaching midnight I felt strangely calm as I reviewed my position. I had weighed everything up to the best of my ability and I decided to accept the Free State demand of unconditional surrender and to appeal to my fellow officers to follow a similar course. In the intervening years I can honestly say that I have never regretted the decision. I made it without fear or favour and in the best interests of the country as I saw it. In placing the facts on record now I do so simply as part of history and I have no desire to discuss the support or criticism of what I did. Shortly before midnight I lay down to get some rest and was soon asleep.

I was awakened the next morning at 4 am by the opening of the door and the switching on of the light. I was informed that my execution would not be suspended unless I agreed to the terms as already stated.

I replied that I was prepared to accept the terms and the party withdrew. A few days later, on 24 January I was taken to Arbour Hill Barracks where I was given facilities to send out full details of my action and a covering note of explanation.

At that time the prison section was half filled with Free State Army prisoners who had been convicted of various offences principally against military discipline. I had no contact with any of these as I was confined to a cell in the unoccupied wing where a regular guard of three officers were my custodians. They were Sean Bolger, Charlie Byrne and Bill O'Reilly. They were very kindly disposed towards me and we had many discussions on a variety of subjects. In time I came to regard them more as friends than as captors. They were the only contacts I had at this time and we established a friendship which lasted for many years. During this time at Arbour Hill I was first presented with a document to sign which would then be forwarded to each member of the anti-Treaty Executive. I was also asked to write a personal document to explain my action and this too would be forwarded to all those concerned. The following are copies of the two documents referred to:

DOCUMENT NO. 1

29 JANUARY 1923

I HAVE UNDERTAKEN FOR THE FUTURE OF IRELAND TO ACCEPT AND AID IN AN IMMEDIATE AND UNCONDITIONAL SURRENDER OF ALL ARMS AND MEN AS REQUIRED BY GENERAL MULCAHY.

Signed LIAM DEASY

IN PURSUANCE OF THIS UNDERTAKING I AM ASKED TO APPEAL FOR A SIMILAR UNDERTAKING AND ACCEPTANCE FROM THE FOLLOWING:

E. DE VALERA	F. AIKEN
P. RUTTLEDGE	F. BARRETT
A. STACK	T. BARRY
N. COLIVET	S. McSWEENEY
D. O'CALLAGHAN	SEAMUS ROBINSON
LIAM LYNCH	HUMPHREY MURPHY
CON MOLONEY	SEAMUS O'DONOVAN
T. DERRIG	FRANK CARTY

AND FOR THE IMMEDIATE AND UNCONDITIONAL SURRENDER OF THEMSELVES AFTER ISSUE BY THEM OF AN ORDER FOR THIS SURRENDER ON THE PART OF ALL THOSE ASSOCIATED WITH THEM, TOGETHER WITH THEIR ARMS AND EQUIPMENT.

Signed LIAM DEASY

DOCUMENT No. 2

30 January 1923

The attachment bearing my signature will very probably be not unexpected but a general surprise: hence my reason for this covering note to you.

Previous to my arrest I had decided to advocate a termination to the present hostilities. My principal reason was based on the grounds that the national position was decreasing in strength, rather than increasing, as a result not so much of the actual fighting but primarily because of the particular side phases that had arisen and were being concentrated on: *viz* the Executions and what followed as a result. That the latter phases would develop and become more intense I had not the slightest doubt, and to avoid our country and people being reduced to such a state I was prepared to advocate a cessation on lines that would mean a temporary setting aside of the attainment of our ideals. To this end I had discussed proposals with a neutral and had asked to have the ideas sent to me in writing. It was my intention to then submit my views to the Chief-of-Staff and if he thought necessary to get the opinions of responsible officers in the area where I operated.

My arrest prevented me carrying out the intentions and it was not until I saw the development of the campaign above referred to, *viz* taking people as hostages because of the acts of their sons or brothers, that I decided to ascertain the extent to which I might go in taking action inside. (Here let me mention that at first I favoured the policy until I saw first of all the difficulties in discriminating between an active person and a non-combatant; and secondly the possibilities of its being the cause of developing a war between families rather than armies.) I asked the C-in-C in Portobello to facilitate my getting in touch with certain IRA leaders through the medium of a neutral, at the same time submitting proposals which I considered would form the basis of negotiations to terminate the war. My request was turned down. Meantime, I was tried before a committee of officers and on the 20th inst notification reached me of my execution on the following morning. I then asked for an interview with the C-in-C and was refused unless I was prepared to guarantee in writing the immediate and unconditional surrender of arms and men, and to issue orders accordingly. I refused to accept this impossible order but agreed to advocate the stopping of the war. At 4 am

I was informed the execution would not be suspended unless I agreed to sign what is contained in Block Capitals in the attached. After long consideration I decided on accepting the conditions in the best interest of the country. The promised aid is contained in the appeal which I now send you and the others whose names have been given to me.

My outlook on the situation immediately prior to arrest was that the fight would go on indefinitely, in so far as our destructive policy was concerned. Government would be made impossible: our hopes of advancing the fight to a successful ending and the clearing up with the English were not however so bright. My hope in this was by the eventual co-operation of the separatist elements in the Free State Army. I was building on the effects, by the Free State Government's policy, on its Army Officers and the results. Since my arrest I have reason to see more clearly the effects which the latter has created, and, candidly I am convinced it has only emphasised the carrying out of instructions even though they are unpleasant. Furthermore, in some way or other most officers get concerned either with the arrest, trial or execution and then when once committed to a thing, even though they may not agree, sufficient moral courage to retract is absent. Very soon it is apparent that every Free State Officer will, in some way, be connected with the executions and then the hope of co-operation is gone. The men are disciplined and the possibility of future desertions is of no avail. You realise the hope I had of eventually making for unity with the separatist elements under the old conditions — the only basis

118

upon which real firm unity can be made — I cannot now from my experience hold out even the slightest hope of a response under present conditions. Only by going back to the 1917 position and working from there do I see a glimmer of hope in bringing about the realisation of our ideals.

In considering the whole position there are a few matters I will put before you all and simply ask that they be carefully weighed before making your decision.

a) The increasing strength of the Free State Army as evidenced by the present response to the recruiting appeal.

b) The decrease in strength of the IRA consequent on the recent numerous arrests.

c) The entire defensive position of our units in many areas and the general decrease in fighting.

d) The 'War Weariness' so apparent in many areas

e) The increasing support to the Free State Government consequent on our failure to combat their false propaganda.

f) The serious situation which the executions have created: *viz* reprisals, counter reprisals.

Regarding a) Undoubtedly the increase is due to unemployment, but then war like the present will only make for more unemployment; in other words more fodder for the battle fields.

Regarding b) In many areas we are confined to the numbers at present under arms and instances of arms being dumped for want of men are not rare. More serious is the loss of fighting officers.

119

Regarding c) Protection of small columns by road blocking, etc. and the impeding of railway traffic is the general rule. Ambushing, town fighting etc. is so very isolated that its effects on the general situation is nil.

Regarding d) This is apparent in the south, and not confined to the rank and file but also among senior officers in our best Brigades.

Regarding e) Comment is needless. This may not be support, but at any rate propaganda has alienated a big percentage of genuine separatists from us.

Regarding f) This calls for more serious consideration than the others. There is nothing to prevent the Government from continuing and naturally reprisals will follow, so will counter reprisals. Then we will have arrived at a point where the war will be waged by both sides against the people, in some cases against active people, but in the majority non-combatants, whose only crime is having a son or a brother in either army, will suffer.

Family against family will be forced to fight in defence until the losses on both sides will be so great some other power, probably England, will be called on to intervene and possibly will be welcomed with more enthusiasm than was displayed on her departure. By this phase we gradually forget the national position — it must be so in a death struggle of this kind. At whatever the sacrifice we must prevent such happenings if the position of Ireland supreme is to be maintained.

I should have referred to the prospect of a summer campaign which will undoubtedly be more intense than was the fight in 1921. You realise what difficulties we confronted in keeping intact during that period. I hope in the foregoing are reasons for ending the present fight. In taking up the stand I have no motive other than for the general good. Fully do I realise the responsibilities which follow the action I have taken. I may not see the end of this — my sentence is only suspended — and I am here as a condemned prisoner; but even if I go there are certain documents written by me when I was thinking only of my end on the night of the 20th which, I feel, will clear my position fully to the satisfaction of my comrades. I also realise the effect this action of mine will have against our forces continuing, but my comrades when they view the whole outlook nationally, will see the absolute urgency of bringing the present chapter to a close: if we conserve our forces the spirit of Ireland is saved. Our advance may be greatly impeded for a time but the freedom we desire will be achieved by, we all hope, our united efforts again.

Only because I believe this fight will eventually end in negotiations do I make this appeal. A suspension of executions until the 6th February is guaranteed. Your reply to the attached is expected by that date, or as soon after as you have had an opportunity of considering fully the whole matter. This note is *absolutely confidential* and is being handed enclosed and sealed by me to a courier appointed by me who will either deliver to you in person or have deiivery made through some person appointed by him. Reply will be addressed to me c/o Adjutant General, Portobello Barracks, Dublin. If you wish to reply in a *confidential note* it can be enclosed in a sealed envelope and sent together with the reply to the attached. I would suggest the sending of replies in the first instance to the Chief-of-Staff and through him to me.

Signed: Liam Deasy

In drafting this letter to the members of the Executive I was fully aware that it should follow on the lines of the unconditional surrender to which I had put my signature. I would also like to add that there was no force either by direct means or by implication from the Free State Authorities at any stage after they had granted a stay of execution on that fateful night in Clonmel.

I was also asked to nominate a friend who would act as courier for me and undertake to deliver each of the sixteen letters to the anti-Treaty Executive. Because of the delicate nature of this mission I suggested Fr Tom Duggan who was then a secretary to the Bishop of Cork and well known because of his efforts for peace since the start of the Civil War. I had no hesitation in entrusting this delicate mission to him. Fr Duggan arrived and was most enthusiastic in his efforts to be helpful. Thanks to his generous co-operation all the letters were delivered to the addresses without delay. Fr Duggan returned to Arbour Hill a few times bringing answers from some members of the Executive including Liam Lynch. All of these gave an unqualified *NO* to my suggestion which did not entirely surprise me. In fact it was what I had anticipated because the idea of ending the conflict would not have appeared so drastic if I were advocating it from a position other than that as a prisoner.

About mid-March I was transferred from Arbour Hill to a wing in Mountjoy which was partly occupied by prisoners under sentence of death or awaiting trial on the capital charge. I was not surprised to meet many old friends who like myself were awaiting execution, but which had been suspended pending the result of my appeal to the anti-Treaty Executive. We considered our lives 'hanging in the balance'.

There was a food shortage resulting in a clampdown on all parcels from outside. Yet, the spirit of the Volunteers did not suffer and without a single exception they were as happy a company as one could hope for, considering the circumstances in which we lived. I was welcomed there without reserve and it was the first meeting with any of my own side since my capture on 18 January. Naturally this brought a happiness and consolation after the strain of recent weeks. Some of my companions wanted to discuss the happenings of the last two months and even to thank me for setting in motion the prospects of ending the War but I ruled it out and appealed to them to await developments in silence rather than discuss something that was so personal to me. They readily appreciated this and the matter was not referred to again.

Among the first to welcome me in Mountjoy were my two good friends of the Black and Tan War, Sean Lehane of Bantry and Jack Fitzgerald of Kilbrittain. With them when they were captured on their way to meet me some two months earlier, was a young man Tommy Mullins from Kinsale. I had already heard of him and of course had known his father, one of our main political supporters in Kinsale, who in consequence had been interned for a long period in 1921/22. The fact that his son was travelling in the company of two such wanted men as Lehane and Fitzgerald had marked him as an important capture hence his inclusion in this select company in this grim wing of Mountjoy. Eight months later Tommy Mullins was one of the forty from the eight hundred prisoners who went on hunger strike for forty-one days.

Here too I met many others whose friendship, established here, continued through all the years bringing many happy hours in the company of men whose association in things national has fostered and encouraged the hope within me that the final goal is still obtainable, and that their example will endure and be followed by future generations. I hope it does not seem invidious if I mention a few of those who made life in prison not only possible but memorable: Paddy Mullaney, Balla; Mick O'Neill, Leixlip, and Bart Hauney, Ballybunion who were part of a column commanded by Mullaney operating in north Kildare. In early January the column was surrounded and all were captured. Of these three Mick O'Neill was outstanding because of his influence as one who always showed a complete disregard for imprisonment and all the hardships that went with it. We all felt that his optimism, courage and good humour did much to make life possible for many who found it difficult. Later on we were joined by old friends; Dan Breen and Sean Hogan from south Tipperary, Stephen

O'Neill, Clonakilty, Dan Corkery, Macroom and Maurice Twomey, Fermoy. For me the joy of meeting Sean Lehane and Jack Fitzgerald was short lived when the policy of executions and reprisals was resumed. If anything this vendetta was waged with what seemed an unbelievable viciousness. The tragedies of Ballyseedy, Countess Bridge and Cahirciveen in Kerry following the killing of a Free State officer in a trap mine in Knocknagoshel; the execution of Charlie Daly and three companions in Dromboe Castle in Donegal and a number of others through the country was climaxed by the tragedy of Clashmealcon Caves in Kerry in mid-April where 'Aero' Lyons and five companions were killed. When a Cabinet Minister was publicly questioned about the seventy-seven executions his reply was: 'And seventy-seven more if necessary.'

The country had sunken to the lowest depths in its long history.

Finally on the 10 April, Liam Lynch was killed on the northern slopes of the Knockmealdown mountains near Newcastle in south Tipperary. Then all was gloom but a few days later came relief when it was announced that the anti-Treaty Government and the Executive had ended the war by a cease-fire order as from Monday 30 April 1923. Looking back on it now the feeling among us prisoners was concerned not so much with what the conditions of the cease-fire might be be but rather relief that the War had ended. We had experienced ten months of Ireland's greatest tragedy and now at the end, in my opinion, 99% of those responsible on both sides would breathe a fervent

'Thank God' while almost all of the people throughout the country would reiterate these words of thanks and relief.

Undoubtedly the news presaged a military defeat for our forces but on this same date seven years previously the forces of the Republic had surrendered to overwhelming British forces in Dublin and just as the leaders of that time saw not the end of a dream but merely a prelude to the resurgence of the Spirit of Ireland, we too felt that even in this bitter defeat we had advanced another step towards Ireland free and undivided.

Harry Boland: A Biography

Jim Maher

This is the first modern biography of a man who has been best known as a comrade and confidant – as well as rival in love – of Michael Collins.

As a member of the Irish Republican Brotherhood (IRB), Boland took part in the 1916 Rising and after his release from prison was appointed secretary to Sinn Féin. He played a prominent role in demanding political status for Irish prisoners in Britain. With Michael Collins he helped to build up the IRB and the Volunteers and organised the escape of Éamon de Valera from Lincoln Prison.

This volume gives a more comprehensive review of the six months prior to the Civl War (January to June 1922) than any previous publication. Boland's tragic death in the early days of the Civil War has gone down in popular history but this is the first time that the story of his last years and months has been fully told.

Jim Maher has spent many years researching the Civil War. He is also the author of a book on the War of Independence, *The Flying Columns – West Kilkenny*.

MERCIER PRESS

WHEN THE NORMANS CAME TO IRELAND

MAURICE SHEEHY

When the Normans came to Ireland they established a political structure that was to last almost eight centuries. At no time during that long period did the political structure even loosely reflect the native identity.

The Ireland into which the Anglo-Norman crusade came in the twelfth century was culturally isolated from the rest of the world. The contemporary description of the Irish as an alien people represents not only the view from the nighbouring island but also the opinion of leading European administrators who come into contact with them. The crusade that we normally call the Norman invasion was a distinctly Christian venture. The motivation or justification for the crusade was only slightly more sophisticated than that which sent armies against the heathen during the same era. Maurice Sheehy deals expertly and lucidly with the conflict of cultural and religious identities at the time of the Norman invasion.

Maurice Sheehy, who was a lecturer in University College Dublin, was a classicist, philosopher and expert in medieval Church history. He died in 1991.

MERCIER PRESS